Textualism and Originalism in our Constitutional Republic

An understanding of our Constitution

BY RUSSELL J. RUCKER

TEXTUALISM
AND
ORIGINALISM
IN OUR
CONSTITUTIONAL REPUBLIC

Second Edition

RUSSELL J. RUCKER

ReadersMagnet, LLC

Textualism and Originalism in our
Constitutional Republic: Second Edition

Copyright © 2023 by Russell J. Rucker

Published in the United States of America

Library of Congress Control Number: 2023922401

| ISBN | Paperback: | 979-8-89091-311-1 |
| ISBN | eBook: | 979-8-89091-312-8 |

All rights reserved. No part of this publication may be reproduced, stored in a retrieval system or transmitted in any way by any means, electronic, mechanical, photocopy, recording or otherwise without the prior permission of the author except as provided by USA copyright law.

The opinions expressed by the author are not necessarily those of ReadersMagnet, LLC.

ReadersMagnet, LLC
10620 Treena Street, Suite 230 | San Diego, California, 92131 USA
1.619. 354. 2643 | www.readersmagnet.com

Book design copyright © 2023 by ReadersMagnet, LLC. All rights reserved.

Cover design by Jhiee Oraiz
Interior design by Dorothy Lee

As a schoolboy, I was taught that we had a living, breathing document. It wasn't until years later that I really understood what that meant. That the Constitution of the United States could be bent any way the justices choose in order to make their desired effect. It's like reading the Bible and only picking and choosing what you want to believe. Only to ignore the rest until it's bent into a pretzel and then re-bent and re-bent over and over again into perpetuity.

Any honest person would understand the problem here. Unfortunately, politics got in the way, and not recently. We can go all the way back to the Dred Scott, or Marbury vs. Madison decisions, perhaps even further.

If you're reading this through the lens of a democrat or republican or any other political party, you need to stop and open your mind.

Some people look to the constitution in order to find what they already believe, instead of looking for its true meaning, they're looking to justify their preconceived belief in the document.

This is not an argument for political power as the winds change; actually, it is the opposite of that. It is governing, with each branch of government having the least possible power. This is simply an explanation of what is, and the why.

So here we are!

That's why textualism is so important; you know, when you actually read the text and believe it's what it says it is. Judges do this every month when they read the statutes, understand what it says, and then simply follow the law and apply it. At least they should! Pretty easy, isn't it. I do understand pretty well at least two of the three branches, as I have served in both the Judicial and Legislative branches of our government.

Originalism is a bit different because it requires an understanding of why things were done the way they were.

I adhere to both textualism and originalism. What the text says with the understanding of why. During the Constitutional Convention, there was much thought put into the rights of the states. There were concerns about the large states over running the small, and the southern and western states versus the eastern states. I will explain further as we get into the text.

I base my statements herein through the readings of the documents of the convention itself, the federalist and anti-federalist papers, letters of the attendees' private letters home, and other documentation.

The Constitutional Convention was intended to improve upon The Articles of Confederation, which were somewhat of a failure on a number of fronts. The weakness of the continental congress for instance to force states to comply was a major issue.

The guarantee of sovereignty and independence as outlined in the Articles of Confederation left the colonies without a general government other than on parchment.

It's this that showed them through their experiences of the weakness of the document itself.

If The Articles of Confederation had been allowed to continue, we would have eventually become separate countries, like Europe is today. At the time the Articles of Confederation was adopted, it was about as far as the individual states were willing to go, but after years of living under them, it was obvious through the colonies the necessity of change, a loose confederation operates without a strong central government, something most of our founders thought necessary.

The Constitution begins with these words known as the **Preamble.**

"We the People of the United States, in Order to form a more perfect Union, establish Justice, insure domestic Tranquility, provide for the common defence, promote the general Welfare, and secure the Blessings of Liberty to ourselves and our Posterity, do ordain and establish this Constitution for the United States of America."

We, the people, the citizens, in order to have a better government than exists under The Articles of Confederation, desire to set up justice, in other words, a fair court system; to have domestic tranquility and peaceful coexistence, in other words, no division, no riots, and the ability to live in peace; to provide for a common defense and establish a system in which we are safe from invasion; and to promote the general welfare, peace, and harmony throughout the land. Promoting general welfare does not refer to our modern welfare state it means each state will look out for one another kind of like a family would look after its other members. We desire to secure the blessings of liberty to ourselves and our posterity; to live in liberty as free men, free of interference from foreign governments, and free to self-govern. We do ordain and establish this Constitution for the United States of America, and we hereby establish this Constitution for the people herein. If you look at it this way, our Constitution is basically a blueprint to set up our government, and the preamble is the foundation upon which we will build a good government.

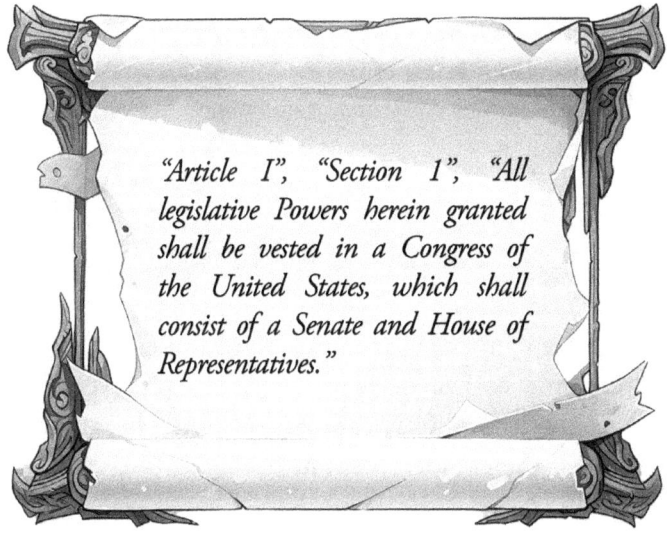

"Article I", "Section 1", "All legislative Powers herein granted shall be vested in a Congress of the United States, which shall consist of a Senate and House of Representatives."

This establishes the two branches of the legislature. One represents the people, often referred to as "The People's House." The other represents the states; the rights of the states. This is the grand compromise between the Virginia and New Jersey plans. There were those who only wanted one branch, and those who wanted two branches. One to be a check upon the other. So goes much of our Constitution where there are constant checks and balances, and it's these checks and balances that make the Constitution so brilliant.

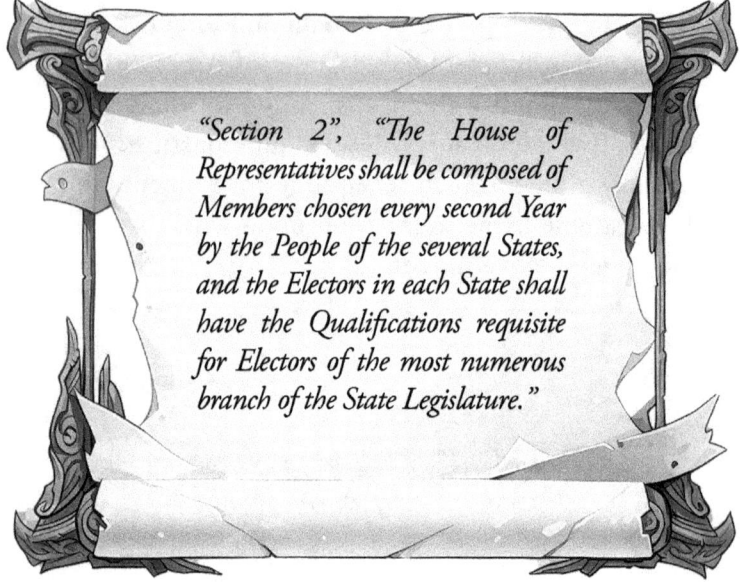

"Section 2", "The House of Representatives shall be composed of Members chosen every second Year by the People of the several States, and the Electors in each State shall have the Qualifications requisite for Electors of the most numerous branch of the State Legislature."

Each member will be up for election every other year. Some of the delegates wanted every year to ensure the representatives were constantly before the people of their respective states.

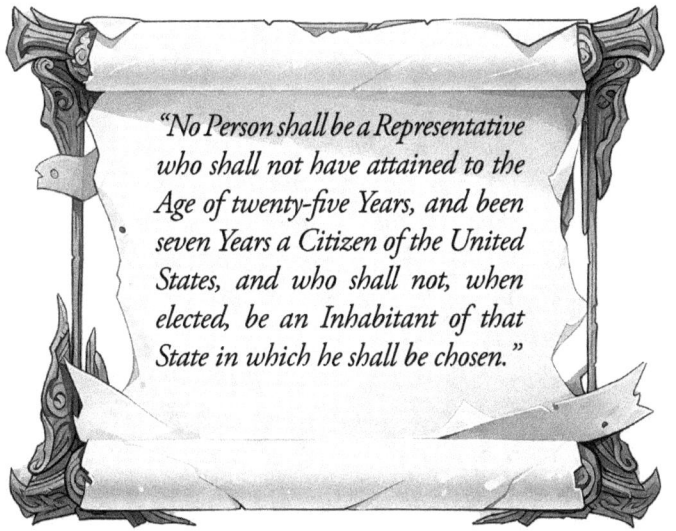

"No Person shall be a Representative who shall not have attained to the Age of twenty-five Years, and been seven Years a Citizen of the United States, and who shall not, when elected, be an Inhabitant of that State in which he shall be chosen."

All representatives must be at least twenty-five years old, to ensure a certain level of maturity. They must be a citizen for at least seven years to ensure they are a loyal citizen. They must be an inhabitant of the state where they reside to ensure they live amongst the people they will represent. And they must have the qualifications for office required at the state level.

"Representatives and direct Taxes shall be apportioned among the several States which may be included within this Union, according to their respective Numbers, which shall be determined by adding to the whole Number of free Persons, including those bound to Service for a Term of Years and excluding Indians not taxed, three fifths of all other Persons. The actual Enumeration shall be made within three Years after the first Meeting of the Congress of the United States, and within every subsequent Term of ten Years, in such Manner as they shall by Law direct. The number of Representatives shall not exceed one for every thirty Thousand, but each State shall have at Least One Representative; and until such enumeration shall be made, The State of New Hampshire shall be entitled to chuse three, Massachusetts eight, Rhode-Island and Providence Plantations one, Connecticut five, New-York six, New Jersey four, Pennsylvania eight, Delaware one, Maryland six, Virginia ten, North Carolina five, South Carolina five, and Georgia three."

Here we see the establishment of the US census. It tells us who can be counted and the reason being for the purposes of taxation of the states and apportionment of the House of Representatives. State reapportionment for redistricting is so each district has roughly the same number of people represented by a single congressman in the state. The whole purpose of taxation is so the federal government has the funds to pay elected officials and the cost of running a federal government. It also gives temporary numbers to the states for the purpose of representation.

> *"When vacancies happen in the Representation from any State, the Executive Authority thereof shall issue Writs of Election to fill such Vacancies.*
>
> *The House of Representatives shall chuse their Speaker and other Officers; and shall have the sole Power of Impeachment."*

In case of vacancies, the executive authority, the governor of the state, shall issue writs of election. In other words, appoint their successor. The House of Representatives will have the Power to choose all their speakers and other officers as necessary, and it is given the sole power of impeachment. Impeachment is the bringing of formal charges.

"Section 3", "The Senate of the United States shall be composed of two Senators from each State, chosen by the Legislature thereof, for six Years; and each Senator shall have one Vote."

"Immediately after they shall be assembled in Consequence of the first Election, they shall be divided as equally as may be into three Classes. The Seats of the Senators of the first Class shall be vacated at the Expiration of the second Year, and of the second Class at the Expiration of the fourth Year, and of the third Class at the Expiration of the sixth Year, so that one third may be chosen every second Year; and if Vacancies happen by Resignation, or otherwise, during the Recess of the Legislature of any State, the Executive thereof may make temporary Appointments until the next Meeting of the Legislature, which shall then fill such Vacancies."

The purpose of the Senate divided into classes was to slow down the change of power, as opposed to the House where power can change in a single election. The Senate would take six years; it is so cool heads would prevail. Also, senators must be 30 years old, and the House age requirement is 25. Senators must also be a citizen for at least nine years instead of seven for a House member, because it was thought that a higher level of maturity is required to serve in the Senate than in the house. The executive or governor may make appointments due to vacancies but only when the legislature is in recess, and then only until the legislature is back in session. Otherwise known as a recess appointment. Senators are elected to represent their states. The purpose of the senators representing the states is so that in one branch of the legislature all the states will have equal representation, it's a kind of defense of the small versus the larger states. In fact, they were originally chosen by the state's legislatures, although the 17th amendment allows for direct elections. The House is elected to represent the people. This is where the citizens are able to elect their representatives. The People's House.

"No Person shall be a Senator who shall not have attained to the Age of thirty Years, and been nine Years a Citizen of the United States, and who shall not, when elected, be an Inhabitant of that State for which he shall be chosen."

"The Vice President of the United States shall be President of the Senate, but shall have no Vote, unless they be equally divided."

Because the Senate will always have an equal number, the Vice President, acting in his capacity as President of the Senate, will break all ties, and only casts a vote when the votes are tied.

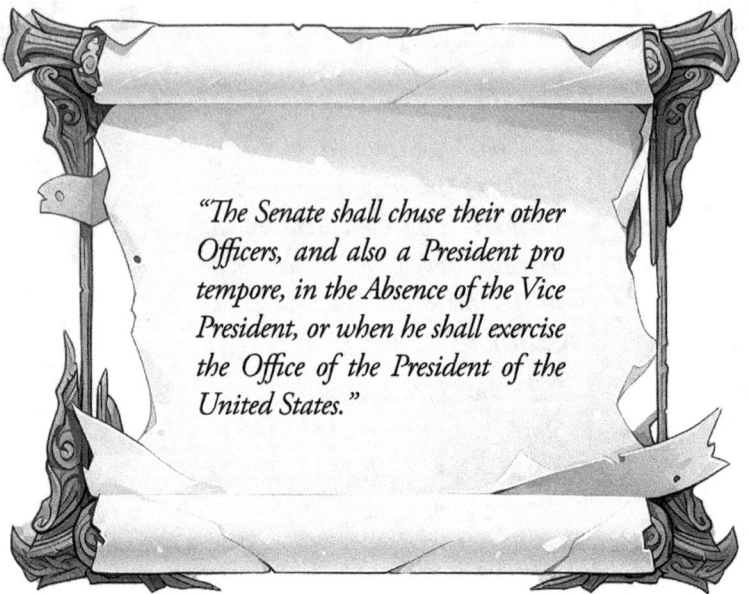

"The Senate shall chuse their other Officers, and also a President pro tempore, in the Absence of the Vice President, or when he shall exercise the Office of the President of the United States."

As does the House, so will the Senate choose their own officers, other than the Vice President. They shall also choose a President Pro tempore to serve when the Vice President is absent.

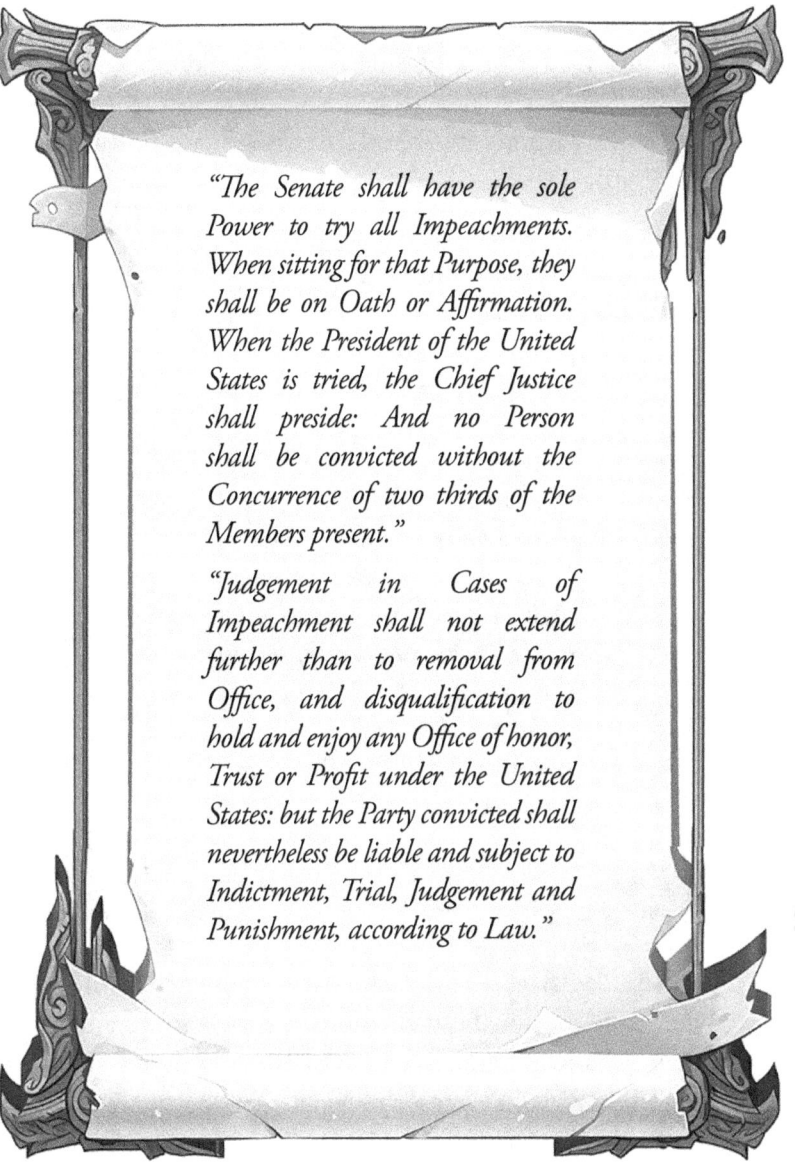

"The Senate shall have the sole Power to try all Impeachments. When sitting for that Purpose, they shall be on Oath or Affirmation. When the President of the United States is tried, the Chief Justice shall preside: And no Person shall be convicted without the Concurrence of two thirds of the Members present."

"Judgement in Cases of Impeachment shall not extend further than to removal from Office, and disqualification to hold and enjoy any Office of honor, Trust or Profit under the United States: but the Party convicted shall nevertheless be liable and subject to Indictment, Trial, Judgement and Punishment, according to Law."

So, the House shall have the sole power of impeachment, but the Senate shall hold the trial, and the chief justice will preside when the President of the United States is on trial. Also, no person will be convicted without two-thirds of the Senate finding them guilty.

The only punishment of Impeachment is removal from and disqualifying the person from holding office. He is, however, subject to conviction for his actions subject to the Law.

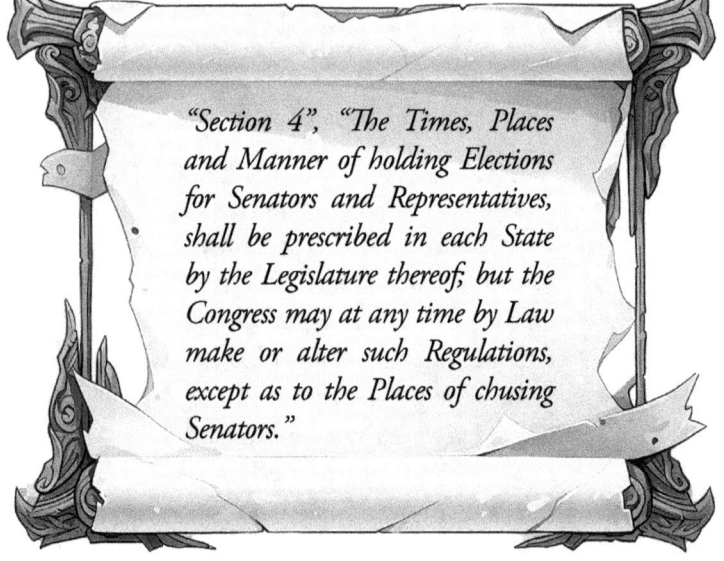

"Section 4", "The Times, Places and Manner of holding Elections for Senators and Representatives, shall be prescribed in each State by the Legislature thereof; but the Congress may at any time by Law make or alter such Regulations, except as to the Places of chusing Senators."

The legislature of each state shall determine where, when, and how elections for the House and Senate shall be held, but it does allow Congress to alter them. It does keep the legislature in charge of the Senate. Time and time again, our Constitution institutes limits on the federal government for many things. Thereby dividing up the power. The objective is to stop any one person from achieving too much power. It should be noted that it gives the legislature in the states, not the governor, the power.

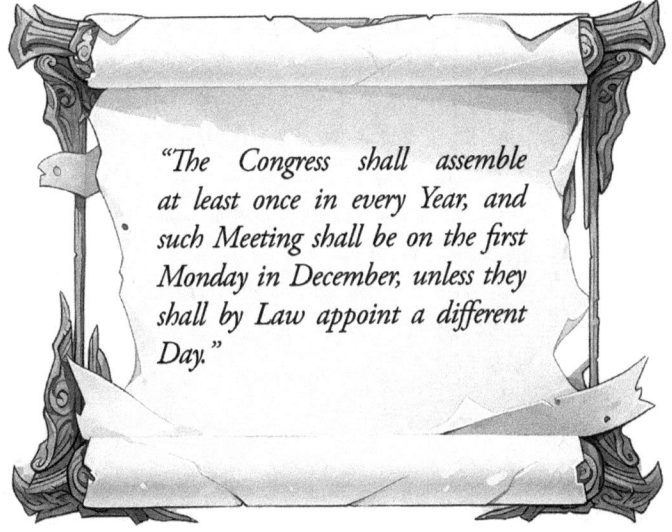

"The Congress shall assemble at least once in every Year, and such Meeting shall be on the first Monday in December, unless they shall by Law appoint a different Day."

This orders congress to meet at least once every year and gives a specific date on which Congress must assemble but does not limit them from assembling again later. It also allows for a different date to be chosen by Law.

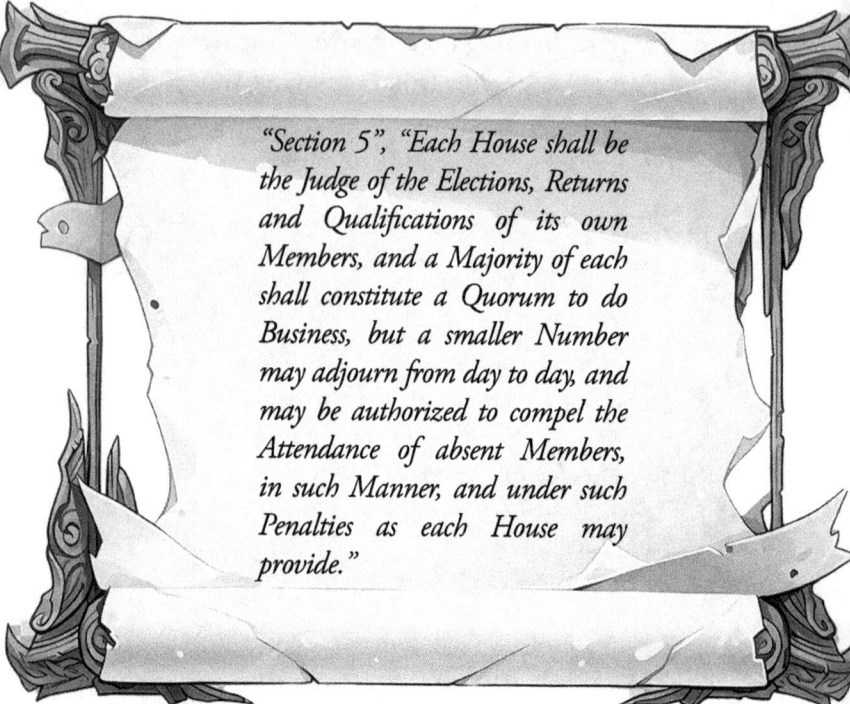

"Section 5", "Each House shall be the Judge of the Elections, Returns and Qualifications of its own Members, and a Majority of each shall constitute a Quorum to do Business, but a smaller Number may adjourn from day to day, and may be authorized to compel the Attendance of absent Members, in such Manner, and under such Penalties as each House may provide."

Each chamber will judge the election results and their qualifications to hold office. A majority shall make up a quorum. However, a smaller number may adjourn from day to day and may compel the attendance and have the power to penalize wayward members.

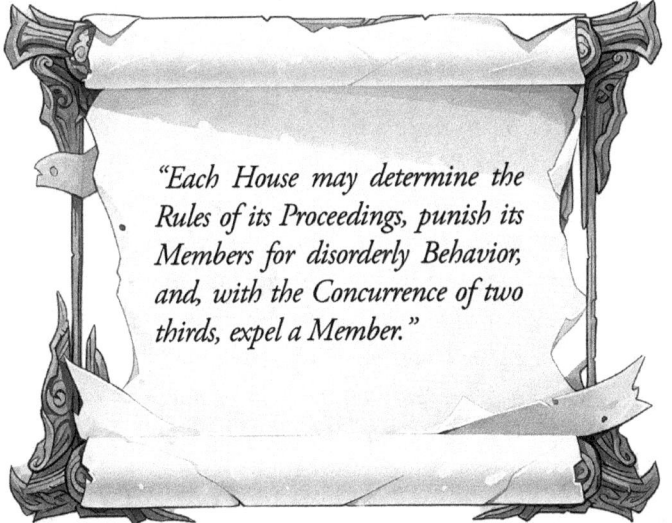

"*Each House may determine the Rules of its Proceedings, punish its Members for disorderly Behavior, and, with the Concurrence of two thirds, expel a Member.*"

Each chamber shall determine its rules of proceedings and punish its members for disorderly behavior. It will, however, take two-thirds to expel a member. Other than disorderly behavior, the Constitution does not give a reason for punishing a duly elected member of Congress.

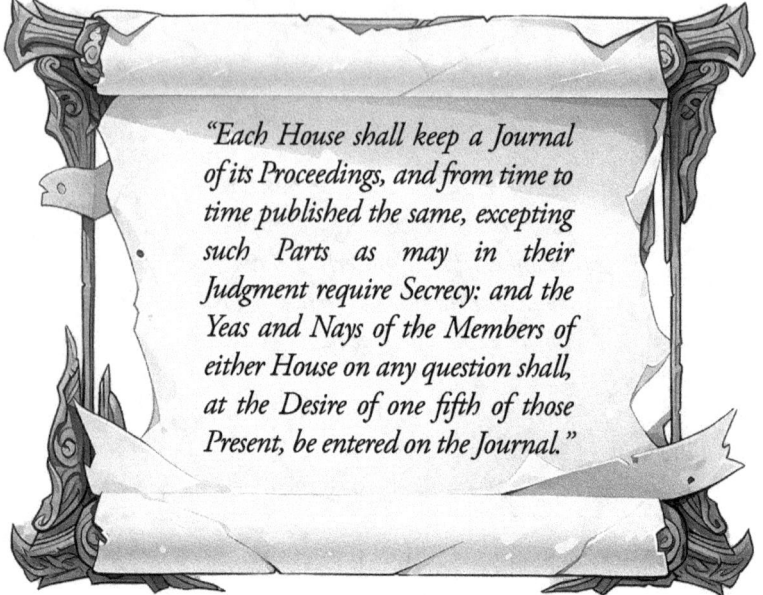

"Each House shall keep a Journal of its Proceedings, and from time to time published the same, excepting such Parts as may in their Judgment require Secrecy: and the Yeas and Nays of the Members of either House on any question shall, at the Desire of one fifth of those Present, be entered on the Journal."

Here, the Constitution orders the publishing of the House proceedings but does not give a concrete timeframe within which the proceedings need to be published. It does, however, order a voting record to be included. The exception mentioned is significant, allowing parts to not be published which require secrecy, such as what may be a matter for national security.

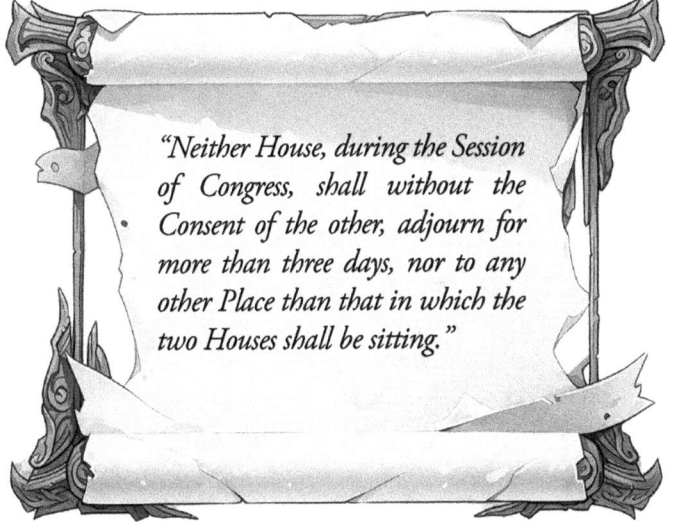

"Neither House, during the Session of Congress, shall without the Consent of the other, adjourn for more than three days, nor to any other Place than that in which the two Houses shall be sitting."

This restricts the House and Senate from adjourning more than three days without the other's consent. It also stops them from meeting in another locality. This is only at a time when Congress shall be in session. Keeping in mind the date was set earlier (in Section 4) in which they must meet.

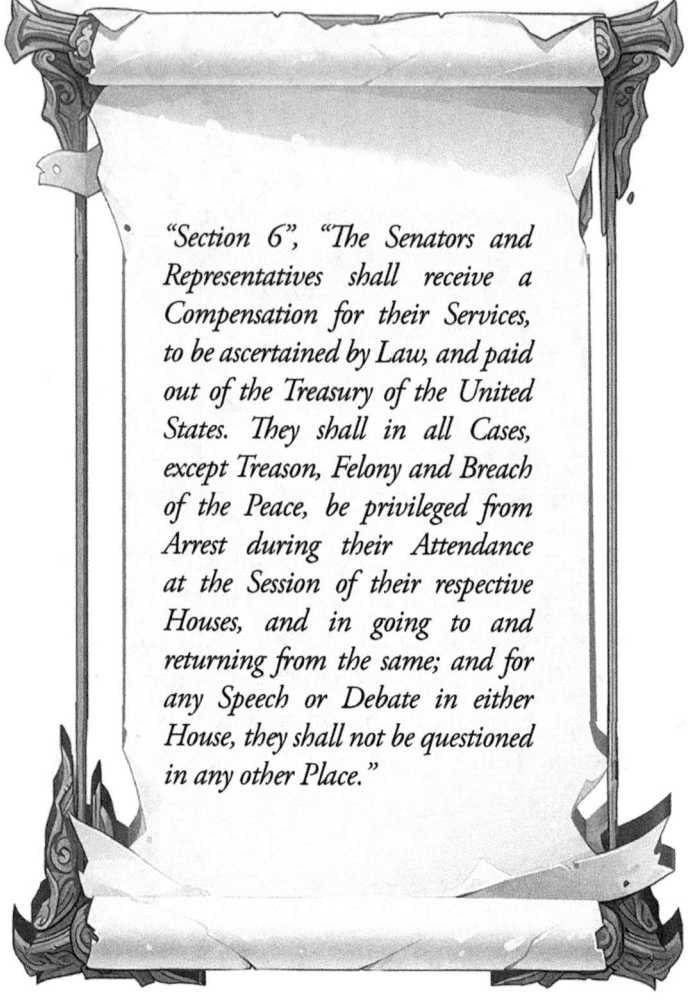

"Section 6", "The Senators and Representatives shall receive a Compensation for their Services, to be ascertained by Law, and paid out of the Treasury of the United States. They shall in all Cases, except Treason, Felony and Breach of the Peace, be privileged from Arrest during their Attendance at the Session of their respective Houses, and in going to and returning from the same; and for any Speech or Debate in either House, they shall not be questioned in any other Place."

This part explains that the members of Congress shall be paid for services out of the U.S. treasury. It also gives them diplomatic immunity from prosecution so the people and states shall not be deprived of representation. However, it gives exceptions for treason, felonies, and breach of peace.

The diplomatic immunity only extends to times when there is a session of Congress or traveling on business for their office. They are not immune from prosecution forever.

> "No Senator or Representative shall, during the Time for which he was elected, be appointed to any civil Office under the Authority of the United States which shall have been created, or the Emoluments whereof shall have been encreased during such time; and no Person holding any Office under the United States, shall be a Member of either House during his Continuance in Office."

No member of Congress can be appointed to a civil office created or where payment has been increased, and no person holding an office may also be a member of Congress. The purpose here is to keep members of Congress separate from all other positions in the government. Our founders were very concerned about anyone achieving too much power. The danger is people getting drunk on power.

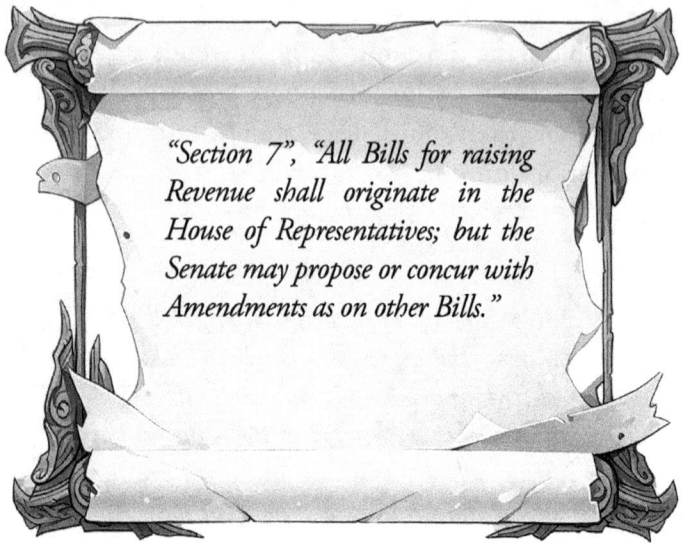

"Section 7", "All Bills for raising Revenue shall originate in the House of Representatives; but the Senate may propose or concur with Amendments as on other Bills."

All bills taxing citizens, states, or in any other way raising revenue must begin in the House of Representatives.

"Every Bill which shall have passed the House of Representatives and the Senate shall, before it become a Law, be presented to the President of the United States; If he approves he shall sign it, but if not he shall return it, with his Objections to that House in which it shall have originated, who shall enter the Objections at large on their Journal, and proceed to reconsider it. If after such Reconsideration two thirds of that House shall agree to pass the Bill, it shall be sent, together with the Objections, to the other House, by which it shall likewise be reconsidered, and if approved by two thirds of that House, it shall become a Law. But in all such Cases the Votes of both Houses shall be determined by yeas and Nays, and the Names of the Persons voting for and against the Bill shall be entered on the Journal of each House respectably, if any Bill shall not be returned by the President within ten Days (Sundays excepted) after it shall have been presented to him, the Same shall be a Law, in like Manner as if he had signed it, unless the Congress by their Adjournment prevent its Return, in which Case it shall not be a Law."

Herein lies the presidential veto power and the power of the legislature to override it. Each bill, after passing both Houses, will be presented to the President of the United States. If he approves it, he shall sign it into law. If not, he shall return it to the House in which it originated with his objections. They shall enter his objections at large in the journal and proceed to reconsider it. If two-thirds agree to pass it, then it shall be sent to the other House for the same; if two-thirds of the other House approve it, it will become law. In all cases, the votes will be by yeas and nays and recorded that way in the journal of each House respectably. If any bill shall not be returned after ten days, excluding Sundays, after being presented with it, even if the President does not sign it, then the bill will become law as if he had signed it, unless the Congress, by their adjournment, prevents its return. In that case, it does not become a law. Here is another example of a division of power. The legislature shall write and pass the bill, but the President must sign it. If he doesn't, the legislature can still override him, which is called a veto override.

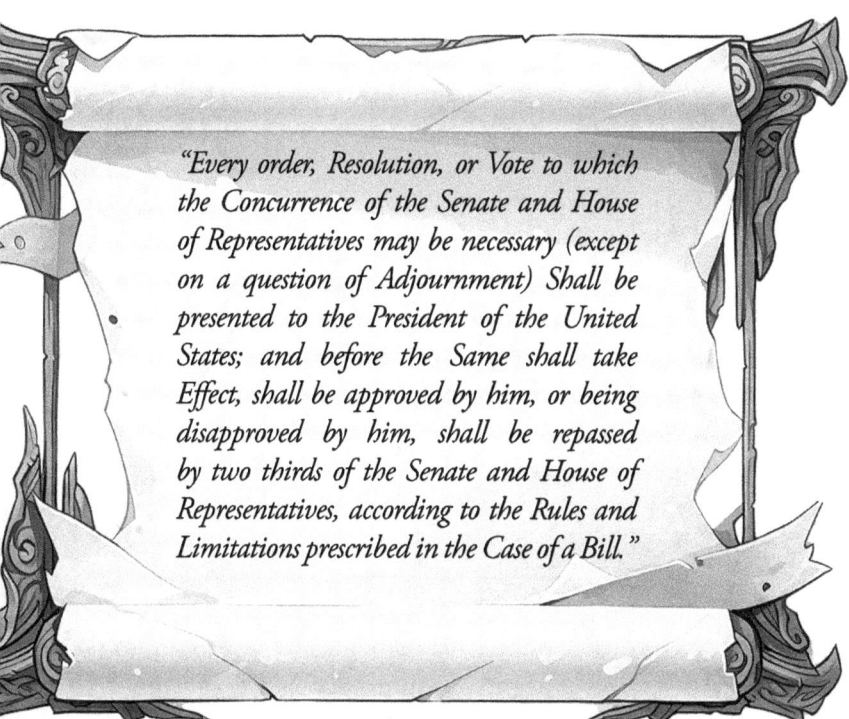

"Every order, Resolution, or Vote to which the Concurrence of the Senate and House of Representatives may be necessary (except on a question of Adjournment) Shall be presented to the President of the United States; and before the Same shall take Effect, shall be approved by him, or being disapproved by him, shall be repassed by two thirds of the Senate and House of Representatives, according to the Rules and Limitations prescribed in the Case of a Bill."

This forces presidential approval of all bills and restricts the legislature from going at it alone. Once again, it forces two branches to come together for making any decision. What really helped in the Constitutional Convention was the locking up of all information. Vowing secrecy during proceedings forced them all to compromise to achieve their ends. They may not have all agreed in the beginning, but by the time they left, they almost all did.

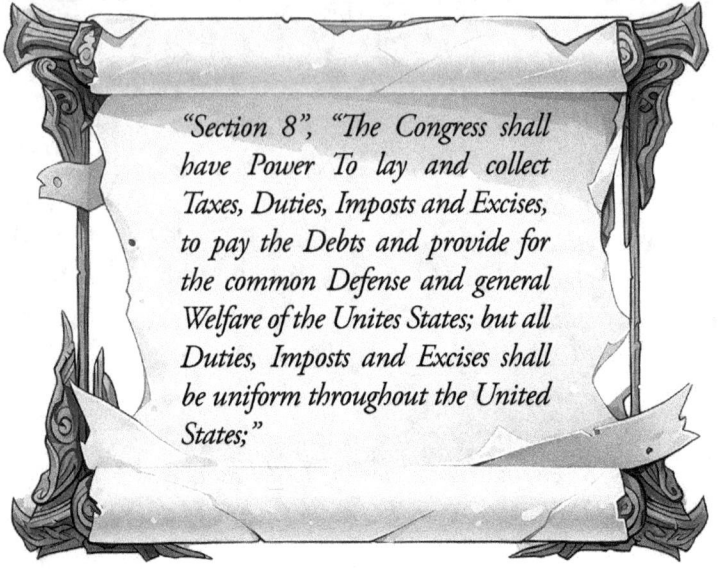

"Section 8", "The Congress shall have Power To lay and collect Taxes, Duties, Imposts and Excises, to pay the Debts and provide for the common Defense and general Welfare of the Unites States; but all Duties, Imposts and Excises shall be uniform throughout the United States;"

Here the Constitution begins to give Congress many specific rights. Among those are the powers to tax, levy duties on imports and excises. It gives reasons for these powers, which are to provide for defense and general welfare. It also instructs Congress to make it a level playing field across all the states.

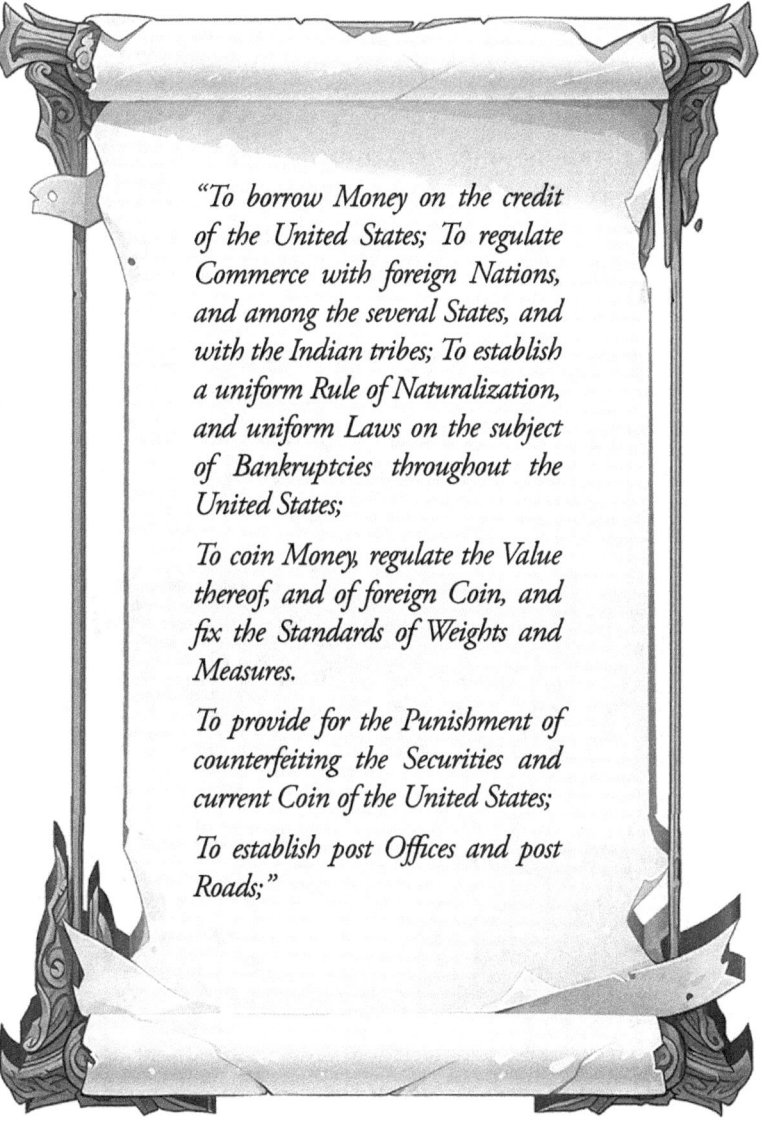

"To borrow Money on the credit of the United States; To regulate Commerce with foreign Nations, and among the several States, and with the Indian tribes; To establish a uniform Rule of Naturalization, and uniform Laws on the subject of Bankruptcies throughout the United States;

To coin Money, regulate the Value thereof, and of foreign Coin, and fix the Standards of Weights and Measures.

To provide for the Punishment of counterfeiting the Securities and current Coin of the United States;

To establish post Offices and post Roads;"

This part goes on to give Congress the power not just to tax, but to borrow money and regulate commerce. Remember, all revenue-raising bills must begin in the House of Representatives. This gives them the power to establish uniformity of naturalization and bankruptcies. They are given the power to coin money and regulate it, and to set standards on weights and measures to provide punishment for counterfeiting. They are also given the power to establish roads and post offices. We are in the middle of a very long list of giving specific rights to Congress. Our founder's definitely thought Congress was the most important of our three branches, yet they tried to equalize them.

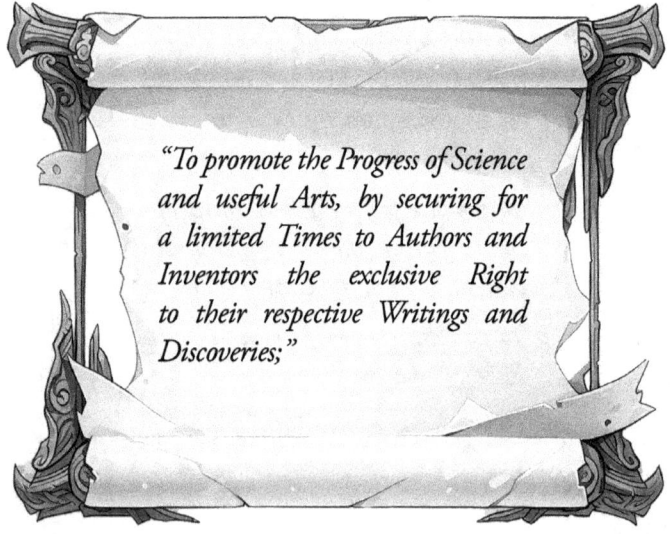

"To promote the Progress of Science and useful Arts, by securing for a limited Times to Authors and Inventors the exclusive Right to their respective Writings and Discoveries;"

Here Congress is given the right to issue patents and copyrights in order to promote Science and the Arts.

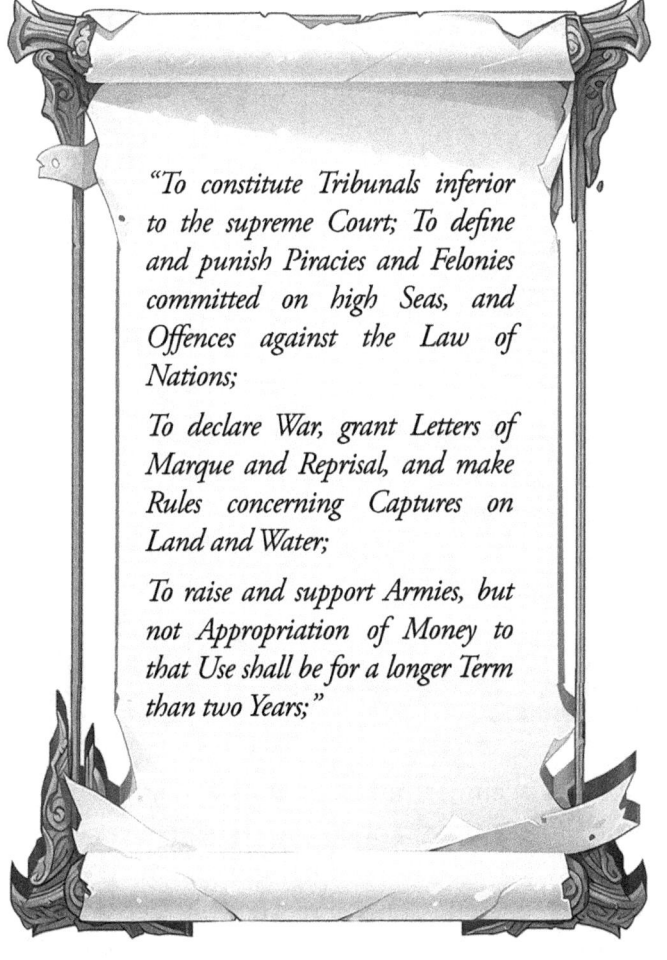

"To constitute Tribunals inferior to the supreme Court; To define and punish Piracies and Felonies committed on high Seas, and Offences against the Law of Nations;

To declare War, grant Letters of Marque and Reprisal, and make Rules concerning Captures on Land and Water;

To raise and support Armies, but not Appropriation of Money to that Use shall be for a longer Term than two Years;"

This section provides rights to set up temporary courts lower than that of the Supreme Court, to define piracy and other felonies committed on the high seas and offenses against other nations, to declare war, and to make rules governing war, issue letters and orders. Congress can raise and support an army but cannot appropriate money for a term longer than two years. So, Congress can declare a war but can only finance it for a two-year period of time. Every two years, a new Congress can re-appropriate funds.

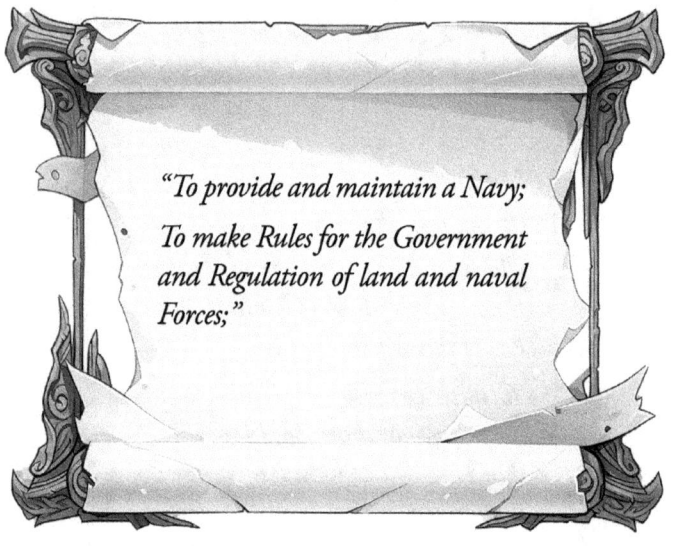

"To provide and maintain a Navy;
To make Rules for the Government and Regulation of land and naval Forces;"

Here again, it puts Congress in charge of the armed forces and the ability to regulate them, but it does not restrict the appropriation of money. A navy was thought to be more important for defense than a standing army. In fact, they distrusted a standing army.

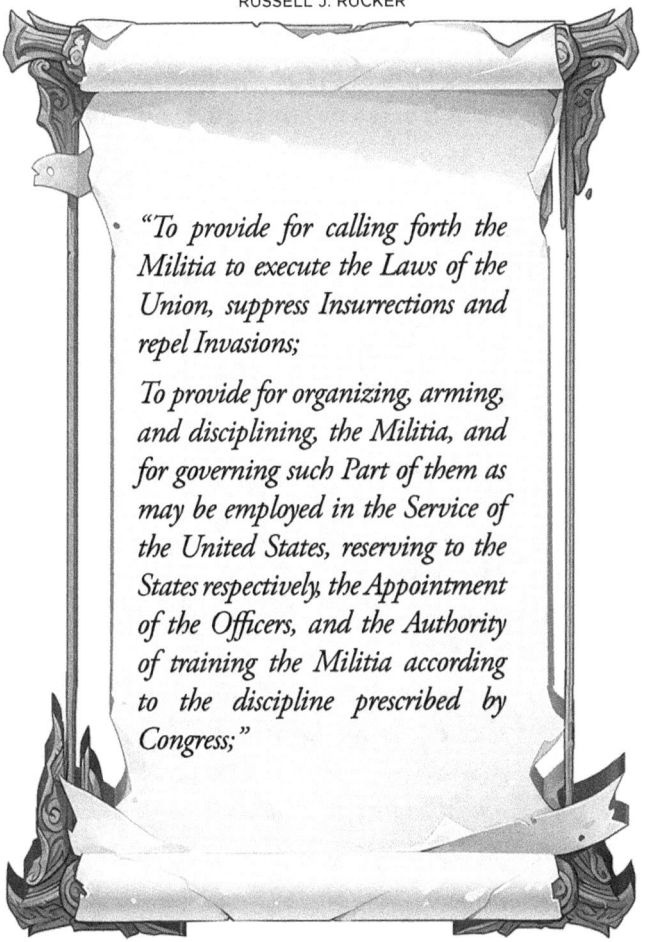

"To provide for calling forth the Militia to execute the Laws of the Union, suppress Insurrections and repel Invasions;

To provide for organizing, arming, and disciplining, the Militia, and for governing such Part of them as may be employed in the Service of the United States, reserving to the States respectively, the Appointment of the Officers, and the Authority of training the Militia according to the discipline prescribed by Congress;"

Here for the first time, the Constitution gives the states' rights. It gives them the power to appoint officers for training and discipline, and reasons for the militia, such as to execute laws of the union and to stop invasions and insurrections. Congress may govern the part of the militia that are deployed in the service of the United States. Congress shall have the right to prescribe rules to appoint officers over training and discipline. So, the States are now sharing powers with the federal/national government.

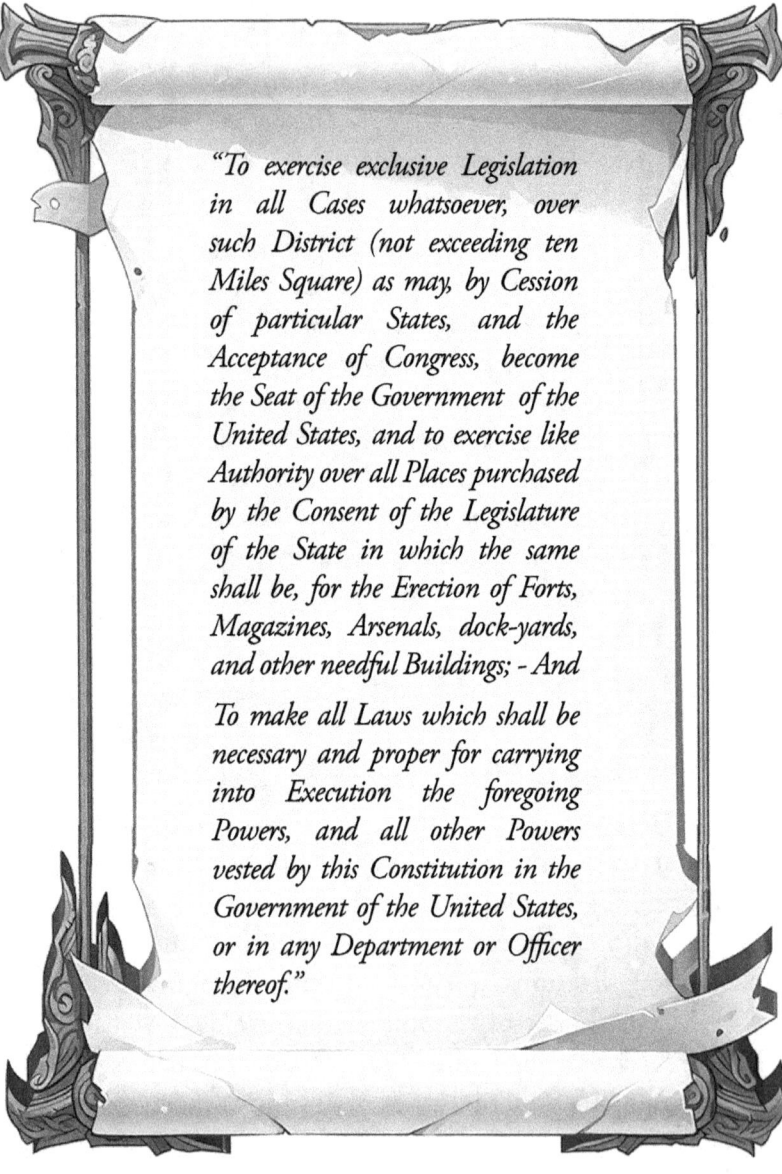

"To exercise exclusive Legislation in all Cases whatsoever, over such District (not exceeding ten Miles Square) as may, by Cession of particular States, and the Acceptance of Congress, become the Seat of the Government of the United States, and to exercise like Authority over all Places purchased by the Consent of the Legislature of the State in which the same shall be, for the Erection of Forts, Magazines, Arsenals, dock-yards, and other needful Buildings; - And

To make all Laws which shall be necessary and proper for carrying into Execution the foregoing Powers, and all other Powers vested by this Constitution in the Government of the United States, or in any Department or Officer thereof."

This part talks about the district to be given to the federal government for a seat of government. It was not to belong to any state. It was believed that if a state had the seat they would be favored by members in government. To avoid it, they set up a district not to be a part of any state. They also set a specific size not to be over 10 square miles and Congress would govern this district.

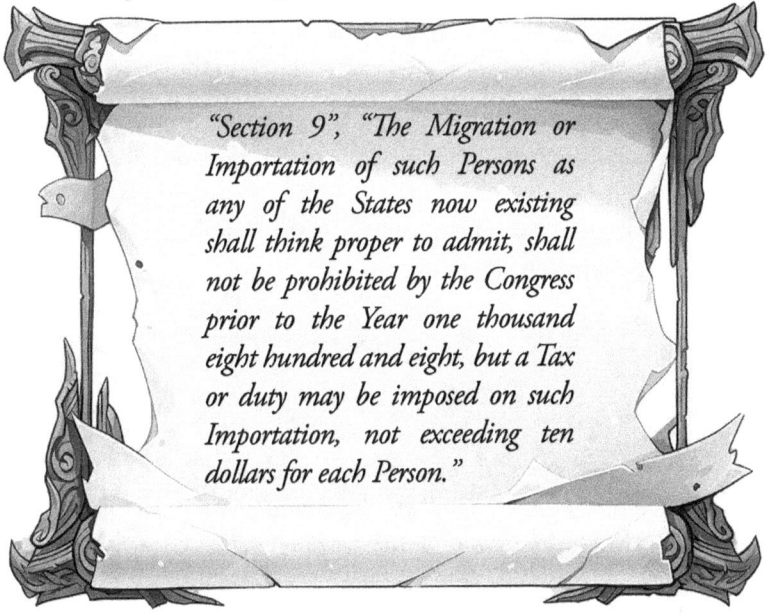

"Section 9", "The Migration or Importation of such Persons as any of the States now existing shall think proper to admit, shall not be prohibited by the Congress prior to the Year one thousand eight hundred and eight, but a Tax or duty may be imposed on such Importation, not exceeding ten dollars for each Person."

This prohibits Congress from ending slavery until 1808. This was to protect Georgia and South Carolina, which they were in fear of the possibility of them not signing off on the Constitution due to slavery.

"The Privilege of the Writ of Habeas Corpus shall not be suspended, unless when in Cases of Rebellion or Invasion the public Safety may require it."

This is a guarantee of the rights of the accused from prison without trial.

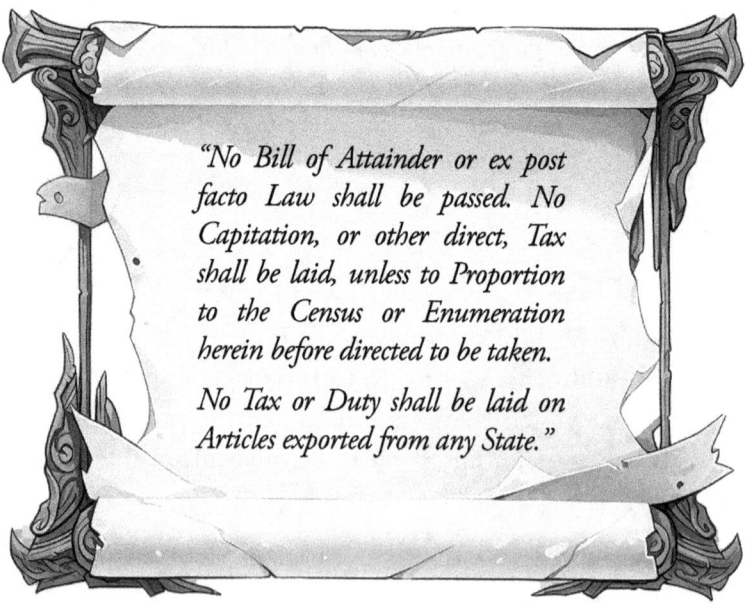

"No Bill of Attainder or ex post facto Law shall be passed. No Capitation, or other direct, Tax shall be laid, unless to Proportion to the Census or Enumeration herein before directed to be taken.

No Tax or Duty shall be laid on Articles exported from any State."

This protects states from a direct tax on persons other than through census or enumeration. Basically, protecting the slave states.

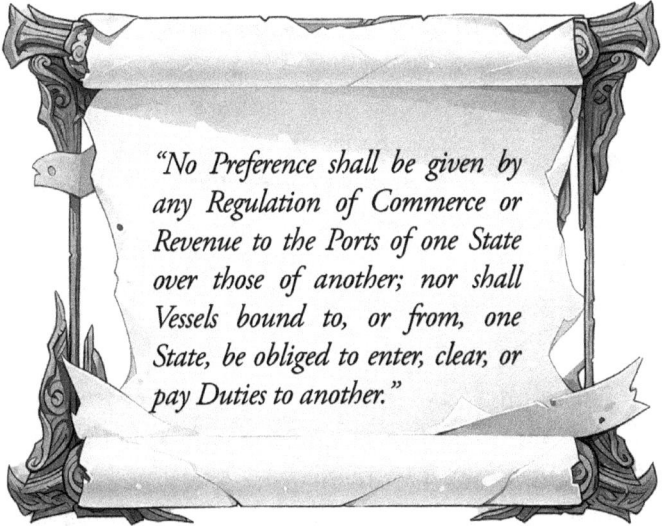

"No Preference shall be given by any Regulation of Commerce or Revenue to the Ports of one State over those of another; nor shall Vessels bound to, or from, one State, be obliged to enter, clear, or pay Duties to another."

All imports and exports shall be treated equally between the states. States cannot impose a tax or duty between states.

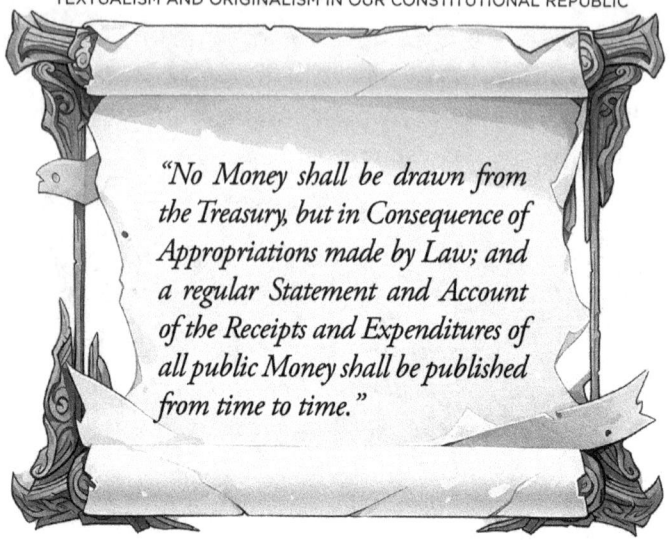

No money can be spent from the treasury without the weight of law, and a regular statement of accounting must be made.

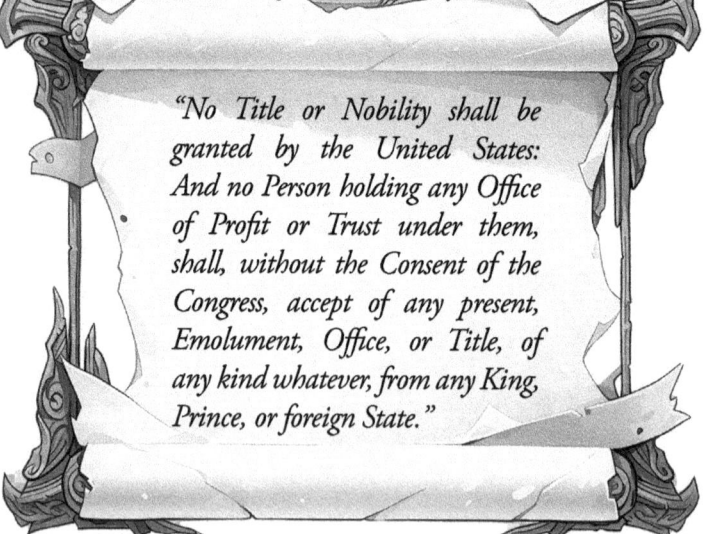

No person may accept anything of value other than wages for one's office, without the consent of Congress. This does not mean, however, that Washington or Jefferson could not sell crops from their plantations, hold conferences on their property, entertain foreign dignitaries, or engage in any other legitimate business in which they would otherwise have engaged. It also does not restrict the title of congress person, or senator, or Mr. President.

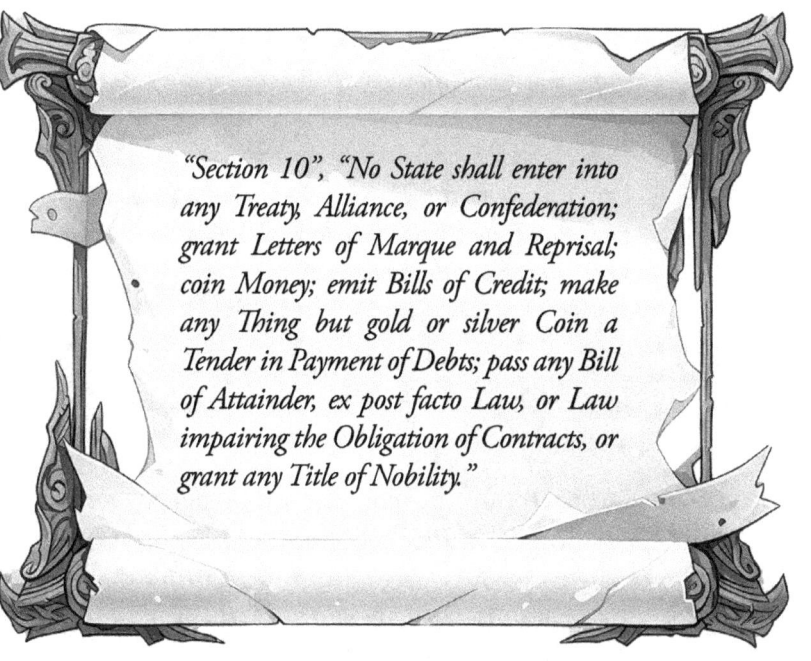

"Section 10", "No State shall enter into any Treaty, Alliance, or Confederation; grant Letters of Marque and Reprisal; coin Money; emit Bills of Credit; make any Thing but gold or silver Coin a Tender in Payment of Debts; pass any Bill of Attainder, ex post facto Law, or Law impairing the Obligation of Contracts, or grant any Title of Nobility."

Here the Constitution limits states from several things. They cannot enter into any treaty alliance or confederation; these things are for the federal government to do. They can't grant letters of Marque, reprisal, coin money, emit bills of credit, or make anything other than gold or silver, accepted as payment of debts. Basically, they can't do anything to undermine the federal government.

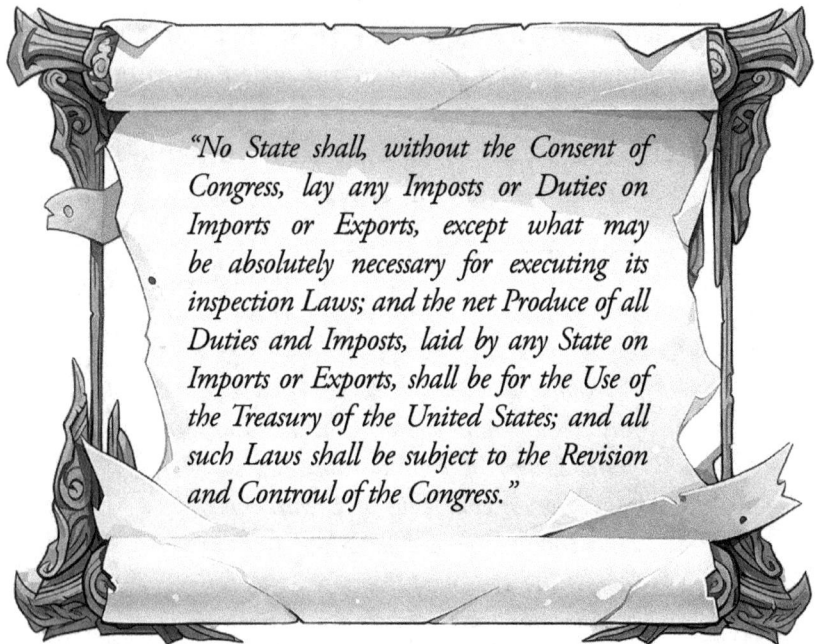

"No State shall, without the Consent of Congress, lay any Imposts or Duties on Imports or Exports, except what may be absolutely necessary for executing its inspection Laws; and the net Produce of all Duties and Imposts, laid by any State on Imports or Exports, shall be for the Use of the Treasury of the United States; and all such Laws shall be subject to the Revision and Controul of the Congress."

A state without the consent of Congress can only lay imposts or duties on imports or exports for the purpose of what is necessary for executing their inspections laws. The net produce of all duties and imposts laid by any state shall be for the use of the treasury of the United States. All such laws are for review by Congress. Basically, we are giving certain rights to the federal government with the express review of Congress.

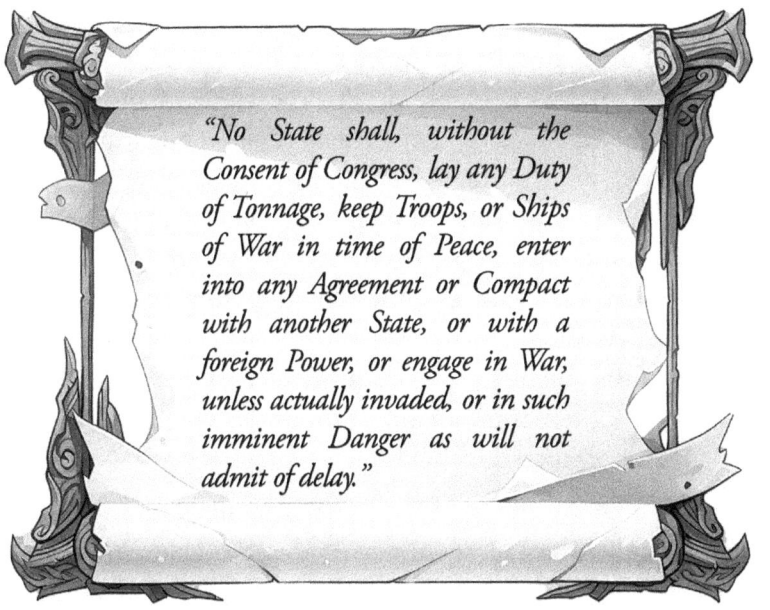

"No State shall, without the Consent of Congress, lay any Duty of Tonnage, keep Troops, or Ships of War in time of Peace, enter into any Agreement or Compact with another State, or with a foreign Power, or engage in War, unless actually invaded, or in such imminent Danger as will not admit of delay."

Here the states not only can't lay duties and imposts, but they can't put a tonnage duty on either. This is the duty of Congress. During times of peace, states can't keep troops, or ships of war. However, it doesn't restrict the federal government from doing so. States can, however, have their militia as discussed earlier. They can't enter into any agreement or compact with another state or with any foreign power. Doing so would interfere with the rights of the federal government through Congress. They can't engage in war unless they are invaded or in imminent danger which they cannot delay. So, the States are allowed to defend themselves in an ostensible crisis until the federal government can intervene.

So, in Article 1 the Constitution gives numerous rights to Congress, as outlined. It also restricts the states in a number of things. It doesn't, however, give Congress a blank check. The states maintain certain rights and have their own obligations. Clearly, our founders thought the legislature was the most important branch, but even there they split it into two branches elected in two completely different ways, doing all they could do to protect the citizenry. They clearly had one thing in common, a genuine distrust of government. They also spent most of their time on the legislature, which shows the importance they held for it.

Some of the executive departments are listed here like that of Commerce, the Department of war /Defense, the Postal Service, the Department of Treasury, the Department of Justice, and the Department of State originally referred to as Foreign Affairs. The Department of the Interior's duties were originally in the department of state. These departments are clearly constitutional as they are within the document. These department heads salaries were paid for originally by the presidents themselves.

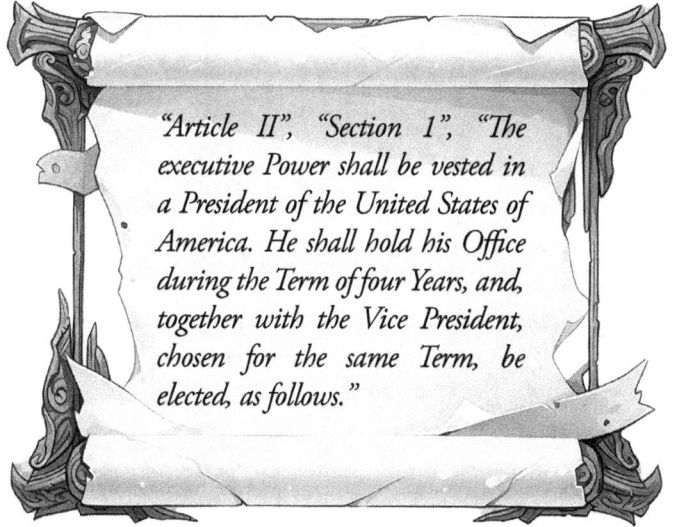

"Article II", "Section 1", "The executive Power shall be vested in a President of the United States of America. He shall hold his Office during the Term of four Years, and, together with the Vice President, chosen for the same Term, be elected, as follows."

Here we begin the discussion of the executive branch, which shall have a president at its head together with a vice president serving together for the same term of four years.

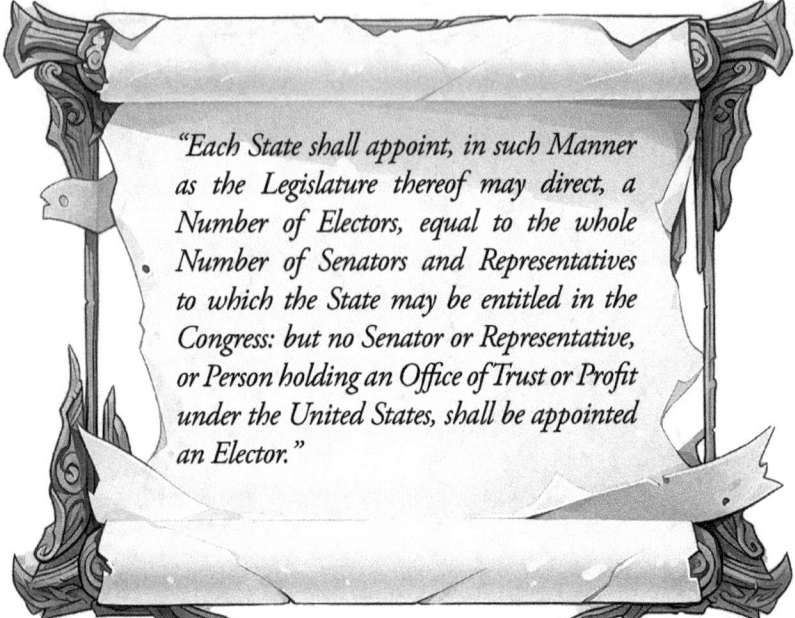

"Each State shall appoint, in such Manner as the Legislature thereof may direct, a Number of Electors, equal to the whole Number of Senators and Representatives to which the State may be entitled in the Congress: but no Senator or Representative, or Person holding an Office of Trust or Profit under the United States, shall be appointed an Elector."

This part forms the electoral college and gives the power to the state legislature to choose who shall be an elector. The number of electors shall be the same as they hold representation in Congress, but no state may appoint their Congressman or Senator for that purpose, not even those who hold any office of public trust under the United States. So, these electors shall be ordinary citizens chosen by the legislature of each state, not the governor. We are again incorporating states' rights here, giving each state a specific number, thereby not giving too much power to any individual state.

"The Electors shall meet in their respective States, and vote by Ballot for two Persons, of whom one at least shall not be an Inhabitant of the same State with themselves. And they shall make a List of all the Persons voted for, and of the Number of Votes for each; which List they shall sign and certify, and transmit sealed to the Seat of the Government of the United States, directed to the President of the Senate. The President of the Senate shall, in the Presence of the Senate and House of Representatives, open all the Certificates, and the Votes shall then be counted. The Person having the greatest Number of Votes shall be the President, if such Number be a Majority of the whole Number of Electors appointed; and if there be more than one who have such Majority, and have an equal Number of Votes,

> *then the House of Representatives shall immediately chuse by Ballot one of them for President; and if no person has a Majority, then from the five highest on the List the said House shall in like Manner chuse the President. But in chusing the President, the Votes shall be taken by States, the Representation from each State having one Vote; A quorum for this Purpose shall consist of a Member or Members from two thirds of the States, and a Majority of all the States shall be necessary to a Choice. In every Case, after the Choice of the President, the Person having the greatest Number of Votes of the Electors shall be the Vice President. But if there should remain two or more who have equal votes, The Senate shall chuse from them by Ballot the Vice President."*

The electoral college is an elaborate system giving each state proportional votes. Each state's electors meet in their respective states, each voting for two people, one of which must be a resident from a different state than which they live. A list shall be kept indicating the votes for each. All this shall be transmitted to the federal seat of government to be opened by the president of the Senate before a joint session of Congress. The person with the greatest number of votes shall be the president. If it is tied, the House shall vote immediately by delegation; each state receiving one vote, the person with the most votes is elected President. If no one still wins, then they will vote from the top five. After the president is chosen, the person with the next most votes shall be the vice president. If the vote is tied, the Senate shall choose who shall be the vice president. A quorum for this purpose shall be made up of members from two-thirds of the states. The states here are given importance, it is not a direct democracy. We are a democratic republic, by contrast. The House represents the people, but not here. This is an election of 50 different states, with each election separate. We are voting for a slate of electors, not for a president. The electors choose the president and vice president. The electoral college was cleaned up and further explained in the 12th Amendment. One of the major problems was the president and vice president would often be of different parties in a two-party system when the top vote-getter is president, and the next is vice president. The Twelfth Amendment corrected this.

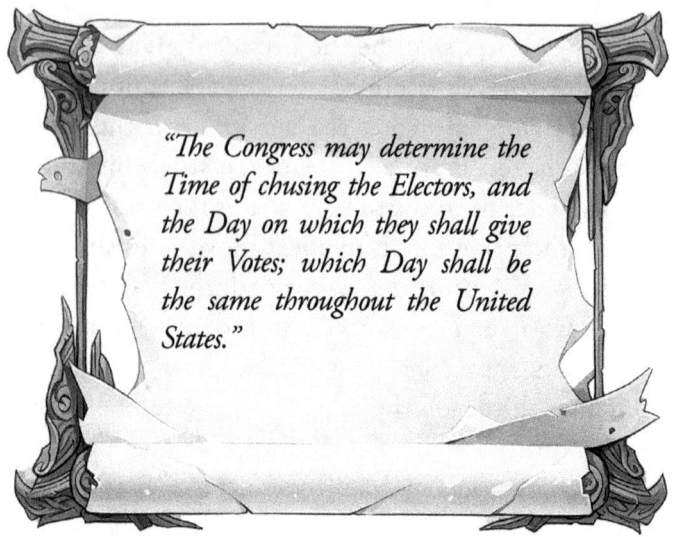

"The Congress may determine the Time of chusing the Electors, and the Day on which they shall give their Votes; which Day shall be the same throughout the United States."

Congress shall determine the time of choosing the electors and the day which they shall give their votes, but it shall be the same throughout the United States.

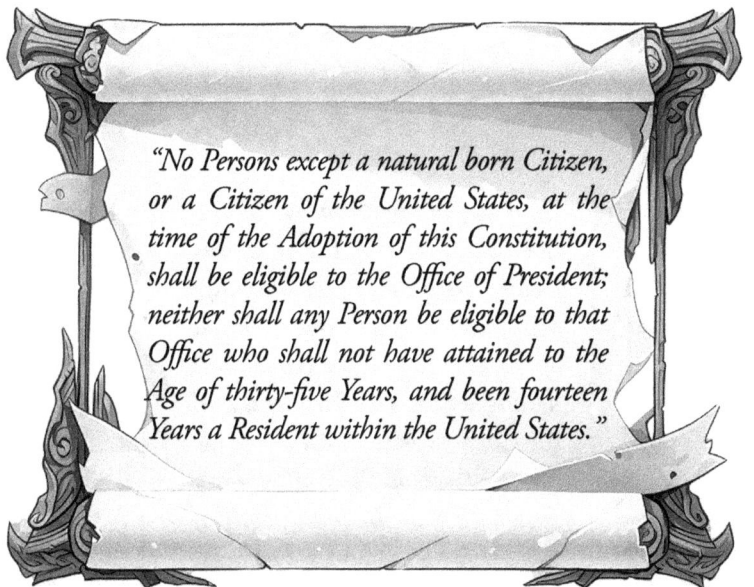

"No Persons except a natural born Citizen, or a Citizen of the United States, at the time of the Adoption of this Constitution, shall be eligible to the Office of President; neither shall any Person be eligible to that Office who shall not have attained to the Age of thirty-five Years, and been fourteen Years a Resident within the United States."

Here are the qualifications to be president. You must be 35 years old, be a naturally born citizen or a citizen at the time of the Constitution's adoption and be a resident of the United States for at least fourteen years.

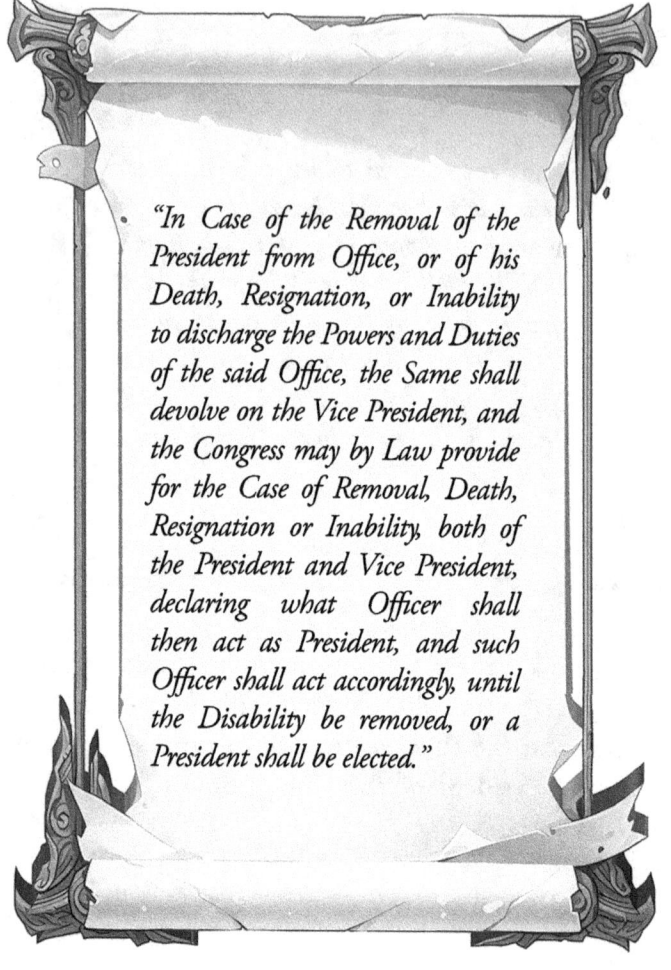

"In Case of the Removal of the President from Office, or of his Death, Resignation, or Inability to discharge the Powers and Duties of the said Office, the Same shall devolve on the Vice President, and the Congress may by Law provide for the Case of Removal, Death, Resignation or Inability, both of the President and Vice President, declaring what Officer shall then act as President, and such Officer shall act accordingly, until the Disability be removed, or a President shall be elected."

In case a president cannot serve due to death, resignation, or the inability to serve or discharge his powers and duties, it would then fall to the vice president to fulfill his duties. The vice president would then be president. Congress by law may provide for removal for both the president and vice president, in which case Congress shall determine what officer will act as president until an election or removal of the disability. It is entirely possible for Congress to appoint someone who is not elected to any office to act as president.

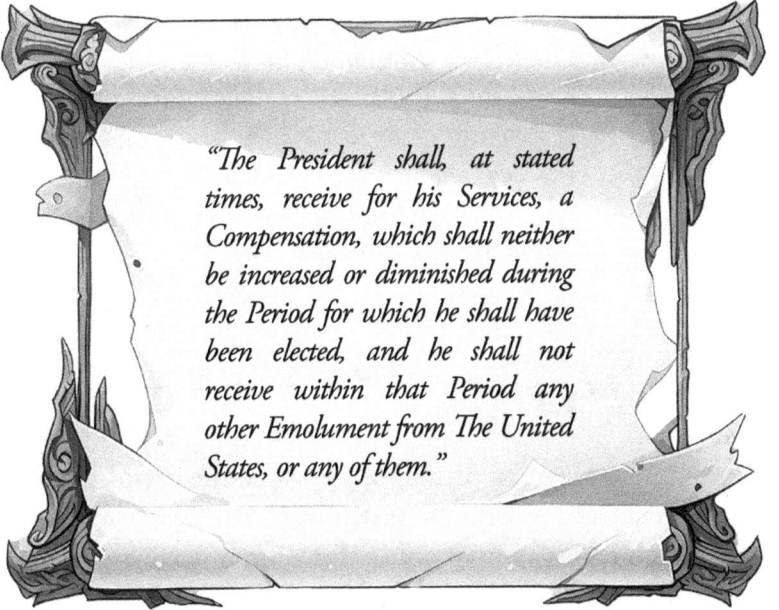

"The President shall, at stated times, receive for his Services, a Compensation, which shall neither be increased or diminished during the Period for which he shall have been elected, and he shall not receive within that Period any other Emolument from The United States, or any of them."

The president shall receive for services a salary that must remain the same throughout his term. He shall not additionally receive anything of any value from the United States or any individual or group of states.

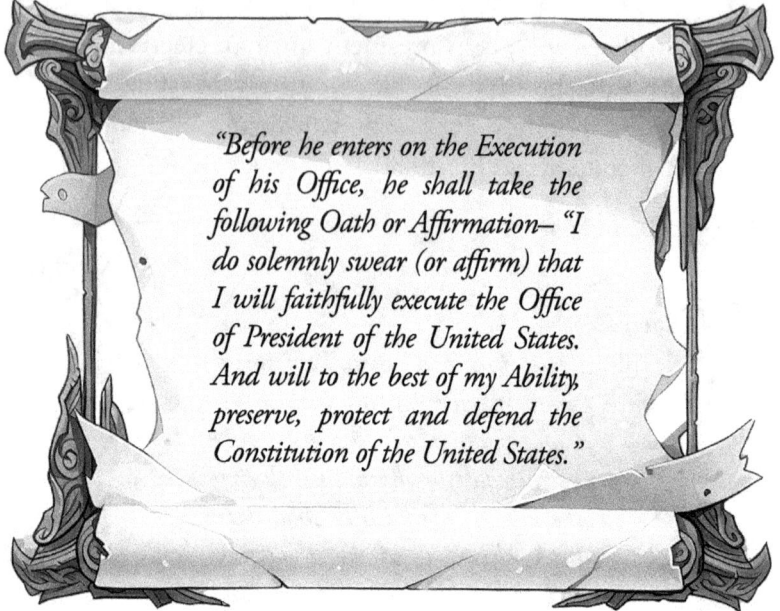

"Before he enters on the Execution of his Office, he shall take the following Oath or Affirmation— "I do solemnly swear (or affirm) that I will faithfully execute the Office of President of the United States. And will to the best of my Ability, preserve, protect and defend the Constitution of the United States."

Herein lies his oath of office which the president is required by the Constitution to say before beginning his term of office. The phrase "so help me God" was added by George Washington as he took his first oath.

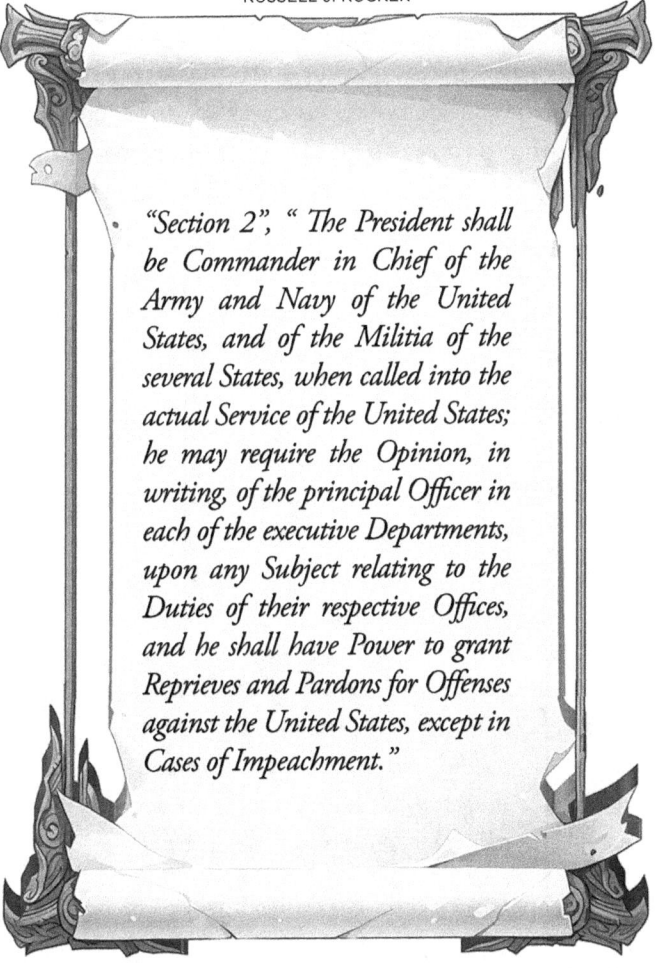

"Section 2", " The President shall be Commander in Chief of the Army and Navy of the United States, and of the Militia of the several States, when called into the actual Service of the United States; he may require the Opinion, in writing, of the principal Officer in each of the executive Departments, upon any Subject relating to the Duties of their respective Offices, and he shall have Power to grant Reprieves and Pardons for Offenses against the United States, except in Cases of Impeachment."

The president shall be Commander in Chief of the army, navy, and the militia when called into service. He does not have the authority to declare war. This requires an act of Congress. So once again, our founders require the branch's work together, not independently. The president here is also given the right to pardon people for offenses against the United States. However, he cannot pardon someone for a crime against an individual state or states. He also does not have that power in cases of impeachment, so he cannot pardon his predecessor once impeached. This part also states that the president may require the opinion in writing on any subject relating to their duties of principal officers of executive departments on any subject relating to their duties.

> "He shall have Power, by and with the Advice and Consent of the Senate, to make Treaties, provided two thirds of the Senators present concur; and he shall nominate, and by and with the Advice and Consent of the Senate, shall appoint Ambassadors, other public Ministers and Consuls, Judges of the supreme Court, and all other officers of the United States, whose Appointments are not herein otherwise provided for, and which shall be established by Law: but the Congress may by Law vest the Appointment of such inferior officers, as they think proper, in the President alone, in the Courts of Law, or in the Heads of Departments."

The president has the power to make treaties, although the Senate must approve by a two-thirds vote of those present. He has the power to nominate ambassadors, public ministers, consuls, judges of the Supreme Court, and all other officers of the United States. The Senate has the power to advise and consent, so the president of the United States must seek the approval of the Senate. Congress holds the right by law to vest the appointment of inferior officers as they think proper.

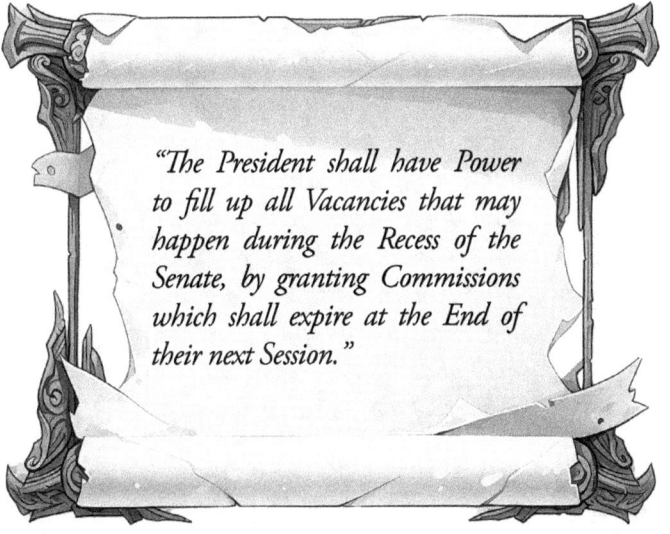

"The President shall have Power to fill up all Vacancies that may happen during the Recess of the Senate, by granting Commissions which shall expire at the End of their next Session."

The president has a limited right to make a recess appointment when and only when the Senate is in recess and only for a commission which will end as the Senate ends its next session. So, because a federal judge serves for life, he cannot be recessed appointed.

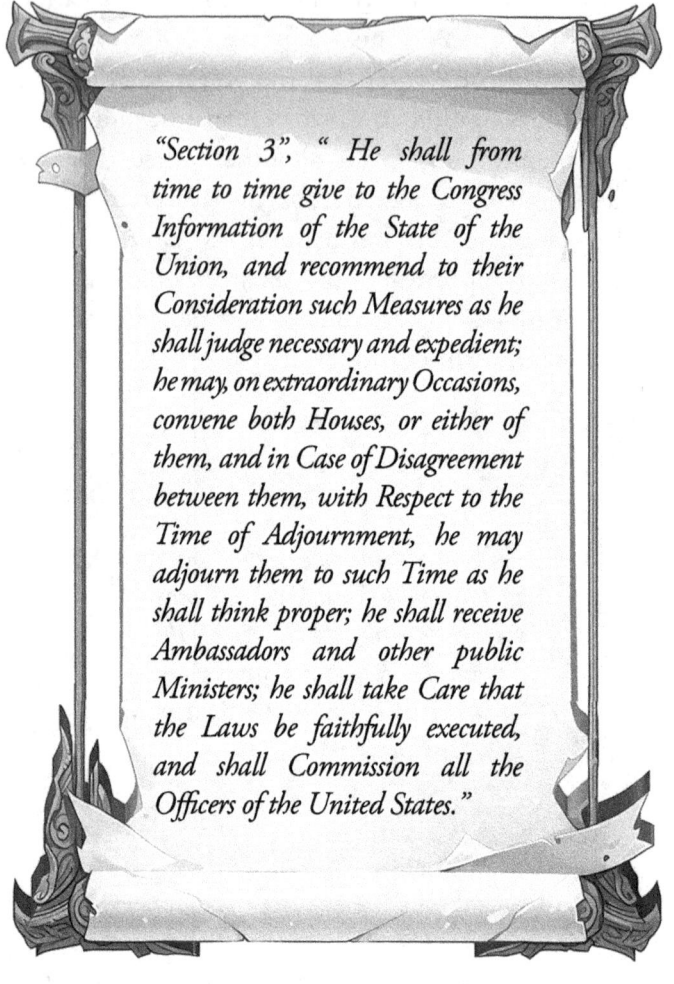

"Section 3", " He shall from time to time give to the Congress Information of the State of the Union, and recommend to their Consideration such Measures as he shall judge necessary and expedient; he may, on extraordinary Occasions, convene both Houses, or either of them, and in Case of Disagreement between them, with Respect to the Time of Adjournment, he may adjourn them to such Time as he shall think proper; he shall receive Ambassadors and other public Ministers; he shall take Care that the Laws be faithfully executed, and shall Commission all the Officers of the United States."

Here the president is ordered from time to time to give to Congress information of the state of the union and he can recommend and consider measures he shall judge necessary. This is usually done by a joint session of Congress for the State of the Union

Address. This was not meant to be a political speech but an important address to congress. He has the power to convene one or both Houses when he deems it necessary. He can also adjourn them to a time he thinks prudent. He shall receive ambassadors, public Ministers, and foreign heads of state. It is his responsibility to see Laws are faithfully executed and commission all the officers of the United States.

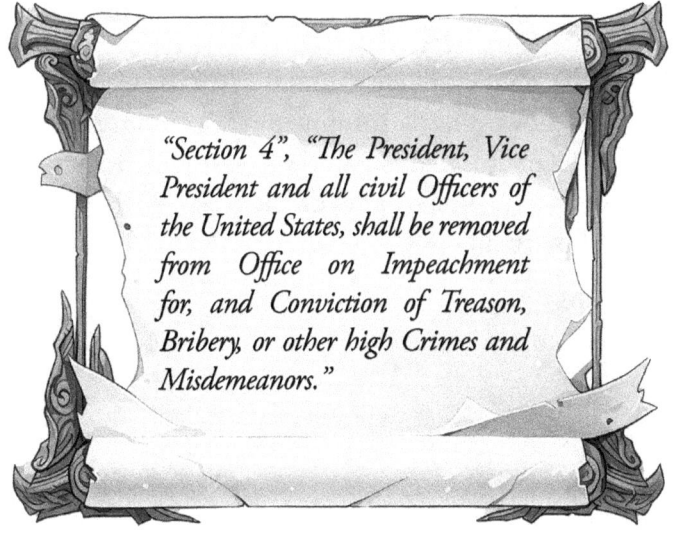

"Section 4", "The President, Vice President and all civil Officers of the United States, shall be removed from Office on Impeachment for, and Conviction of Treason, Bribery, or other high Crimes and Misdemeanors."

Here we talk about impeachment again. The House can impeach, the Senate must try and sit as jury, and removal is only done by a vote of two-thirds of the Senate. But here, it gives the reasons for impeachment as treason, bribery, and other high crimes and misdemeanors. In order for a proper impeachment, there must be a violation of the law. It must be as serious as treason or bribery. Other high crimes and misdemeanors means it must rise to the level of treason or bribery. There can be no other reason. It must not be a political witch hunt. During the convention it was thought that there could not be treason against a state. Rufus King of Massachusetts argued for the term "high crimes and misdemeanors" to make up for this deficiency.

So, in Article II, we have the presidential powers outlined. He has many, but most are shared with other branches of government. We do not have a king. Presidential dictates do not carry the weight of law. It is, however, the absolute duty of Congress and the judiciary to challenge power grabs. If branches of government don't fight for their rights, they will surely lose them.

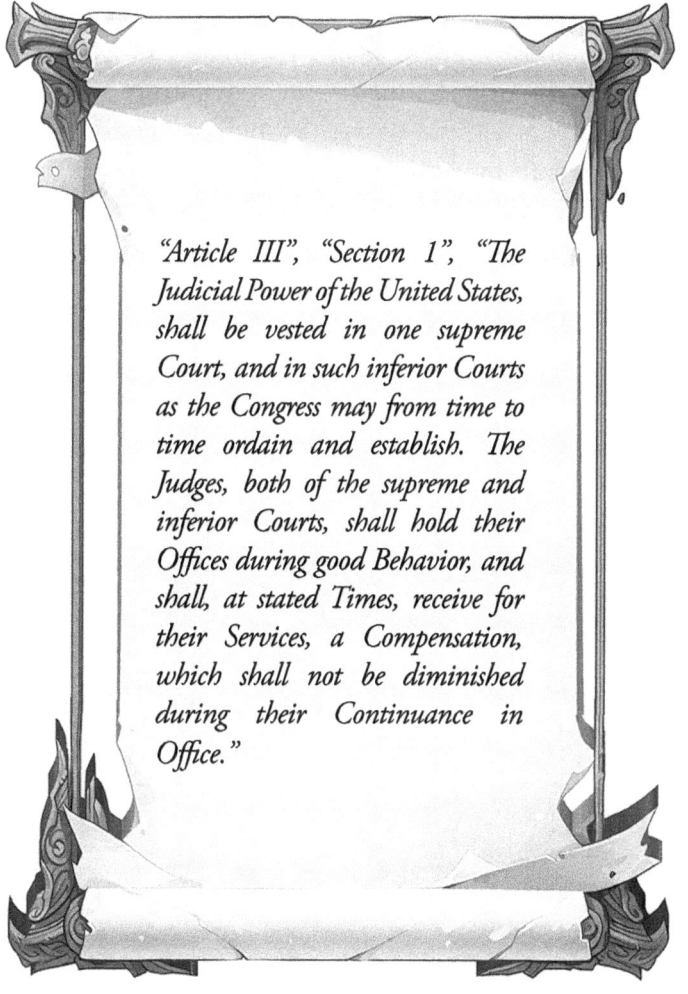

"Article III", "Section 1", "The Judicial Power of the United States, shall be vested in one supreme Court, and in such inferior Courts as the Congress may from time to time ordain and establish. The Judges, both of the supreme and inferior Courts, shall hold their Offices during good Behavior, and shall, at stated Times, receive for their Services, a Compensation, which shall not be diminished during their Continuance in Office."

Here we begin with the final branch of government. The judiciary shall be vested in one supreme court and in inferior courts/lower level federal courts, which Congress from time to time may establish. Judges shall hold their office during good behavior, meaning for life. The purpose of this is so they won't be swayed by public opinion and insulated from politics, as they won't have to run for office. They shall receive compensation for their services which shall not be diminished during their stay in office.

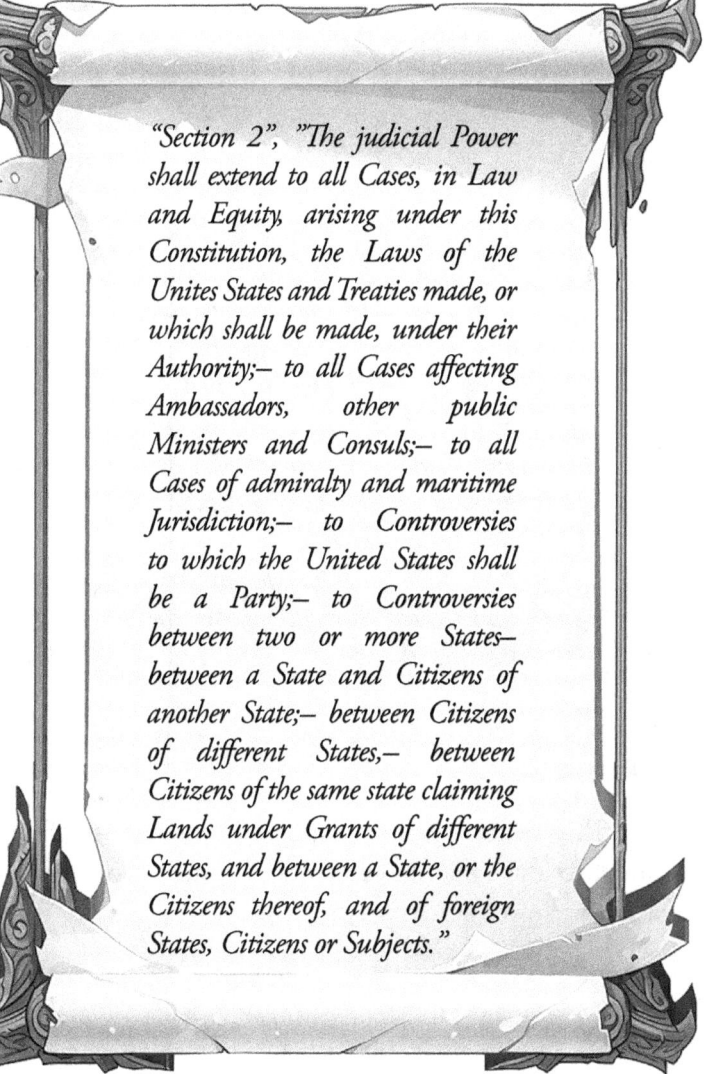

"Section 2", "The judicial Power shall extend to all Cases, in Law and Equity, arising under this Constitution, the Laws of the Unites States and Treaties made, or which shall be made, under their Authority;– to all Cases affecting Ambassadors, other public Ministers and Consuls;– to all Cases of admiralty and maritime Jurisdiction;– to Controversies to which the United States shall be a Party;– to Controversies between two or more States— between a State and Citizens of another State;– between Citizens of different States,– between Citizens of the same state claiming Lands under Grants of different States, and between a State, or the Citizens thereof, and of foreign States, Citizens or Subjects."

This section describes where the authority in cases shall have jurisdiction. It pretty much extends to anything related to the federal government or disputes between states and their citizens.

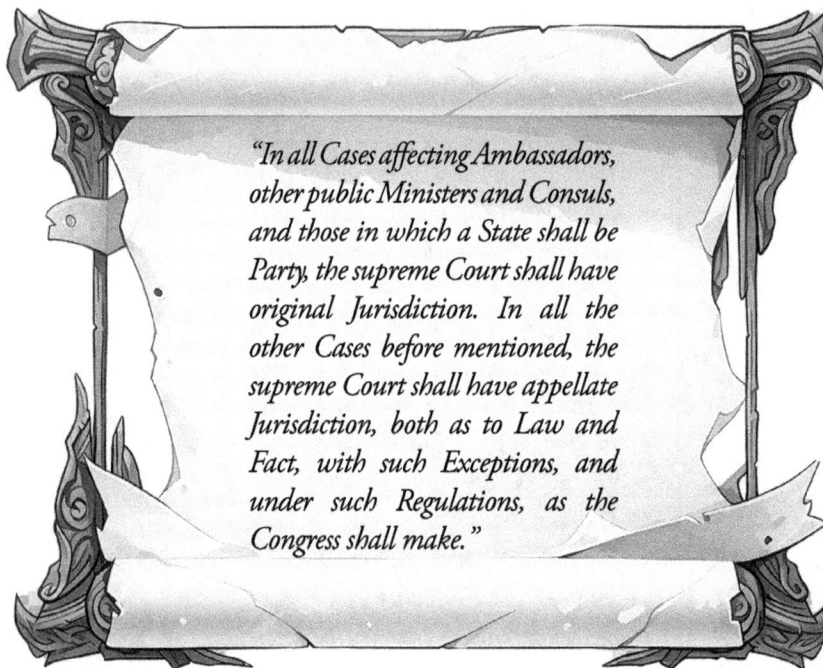

"In all Cases affecting Ambassadors, other public Ministers and Consuls, and those in which a State shall be Party, the supreme Court shall have original Jurisdiction. In all the other Cases before mentioned, the supreme Court shall have appellate Jurisdiction, both as to Law and Fact, with such Exceptions, and under such Regulations, as the Congress shall make."

This section simply explains who has the first jurisdiction, as some cases may rise up through the inferior/lower courts.

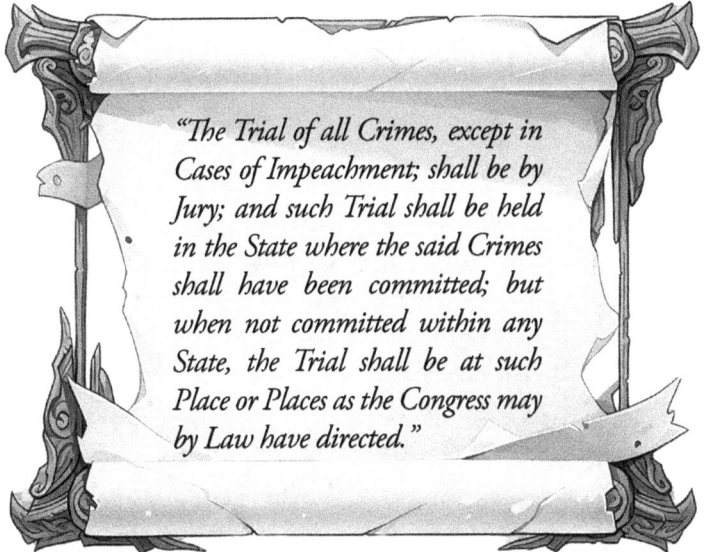

"The Trial of all Crimes, except in Cases of Impeachment, shall be by Jury; and such Trial shall be held in the State where the said Crimes shall have been committed; but when not committed within any State, the Trial shall be at such Place or Places as the Congress may by Law have directed."

Here, the Constitution guarantees a trial by jury. The only exception is that of impeachment. It also guarantees that the trial shall be held locally within the state where the offense occurred. This is also to protect the accused from making it difficult to defend oneself. If the offense did not occur in a state, the trial shall be held where Congress directs.

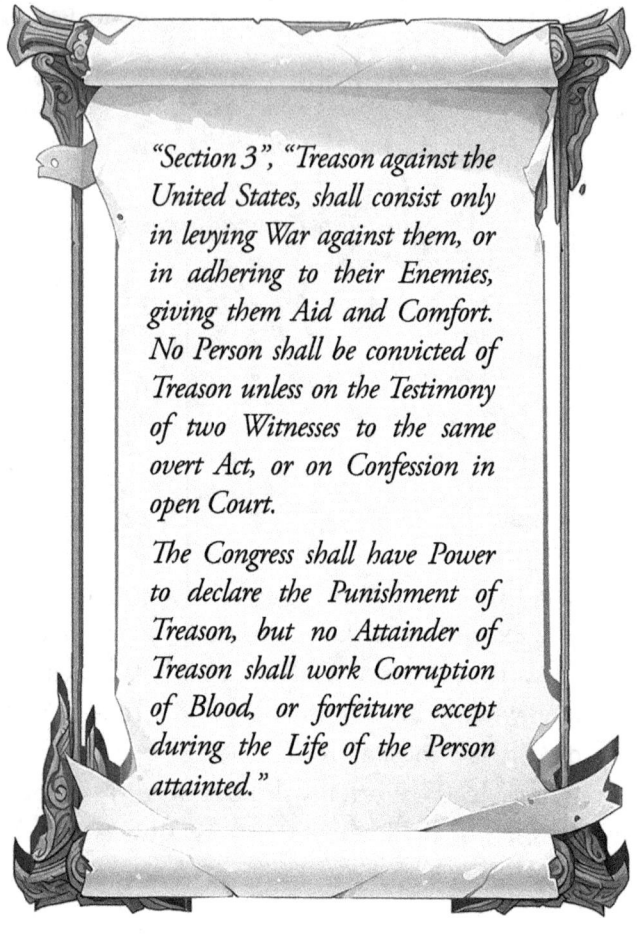

"Section 3", "Treason against the United States, shall consist only in levying War against them, or in adhering to their Enemies, giving them Aid and Comfort. No Person shall be convicted of Treason unless on the Testimony of two Witnesses to the same overt Act, or on Confession in open Court.

The Congress shall have Power to declare the Punishment of Treason, but no Attainder of Treason shall work Corruption of Blood, or forfeiture except during the Life of the Person attainted."

This section explains what treason is, which includes levying war against the United States, helping enemies, or giving aid and comfort. It goes on to state that in order to convict, you must have two witnesses of the same act or have a confession in open court. That is, it! It also gives Congress the power to declare the punishment for such an act.

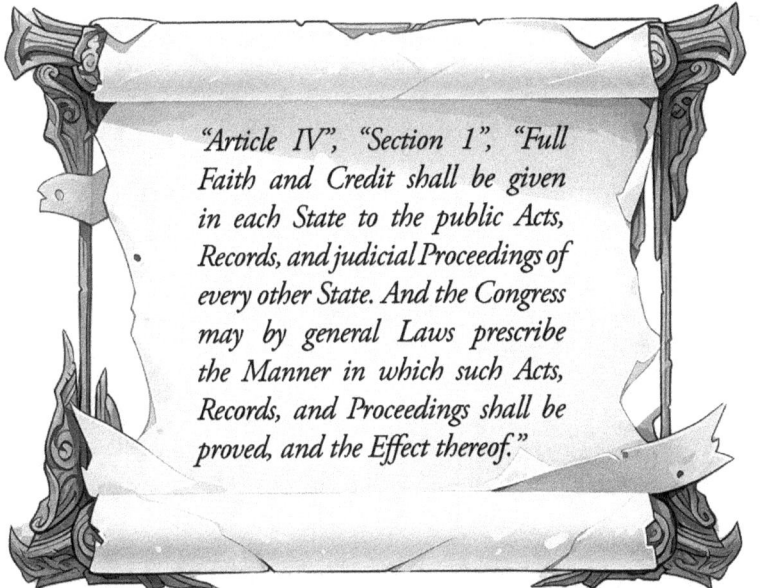

"Article IV", "Section 1", "Full Faith and Credit shall be given in each State to the public Acts, Records, and judicial Proceedings of every other State. And the Congress may by general Laws prescribe the Manner in which such Acts, Records, and Proceedings shall be proved, and the Effect thereof."

Generally speaking, if one state passes a law, it should be respected in another state. This does not mean if a state passes a law, it is the law in another. The weight of a judgement in court carries a higher value in another state than the law. Congress has the power of the effect of the law. So, theirs is the final determination.

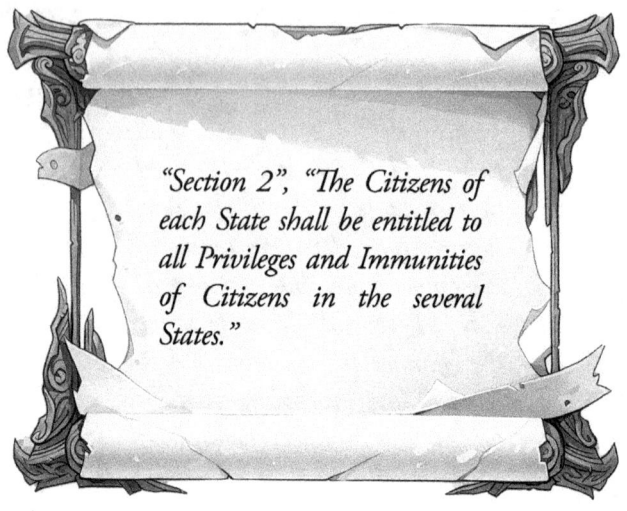

"Section 2", "The Citizens of each State shall be entitled to all Privileges and Immunities of Citizens in the several States."

Citizens shall be treated equally regardless of which state they are in.

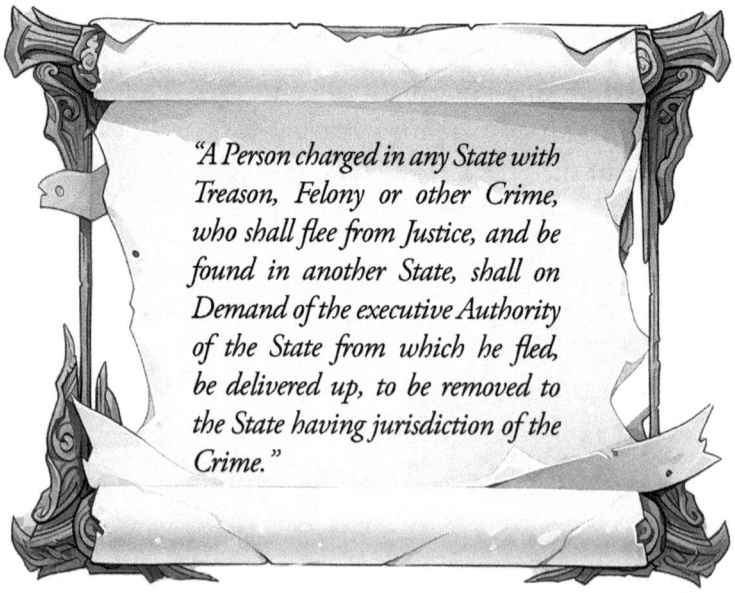

"A Person charged in any State with Treason, Felony or other Crime, who shall flee from Justice, and be found in another State, shall on Demand of the executive Authority of the State from which he fled, be delivered up, to be removed to the State having jurisdiction of the Crime."

This section has to do with extradition. If a person is fleeing justice by crossing state lines, the governor of the first state has the right to ask that he be brought back to face justice.

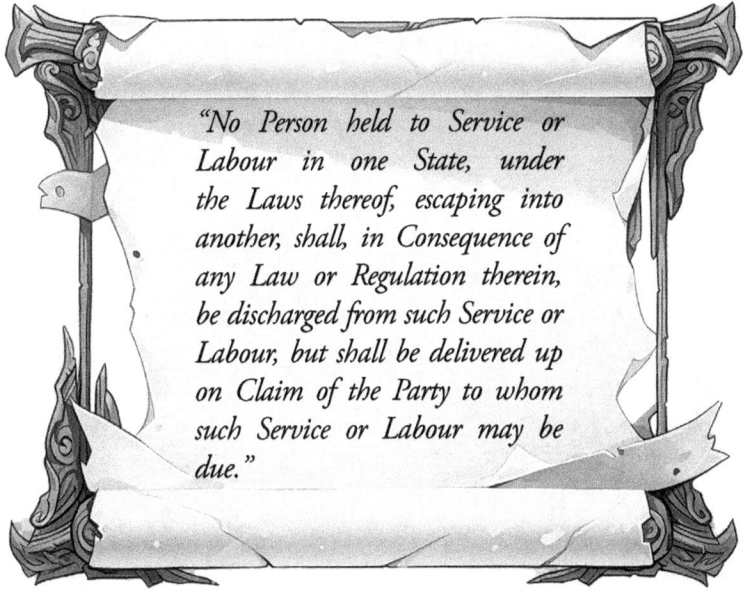

"No Person held to Service or Labour in one State, under the Laws thereof, escaping into another, shall, in Consequence of any Law or Regulation therein, be discharged from such Service or Labour, but shall be delivered up on Claim of the Party to whom such Service or Labour may be due."

No person shall escape from the duty they owe by escaping to another state. I believe this has more to do with the situation of slavery than anything else. However, it is possible to be in some kind of court-ordered service in lieu of a fine.

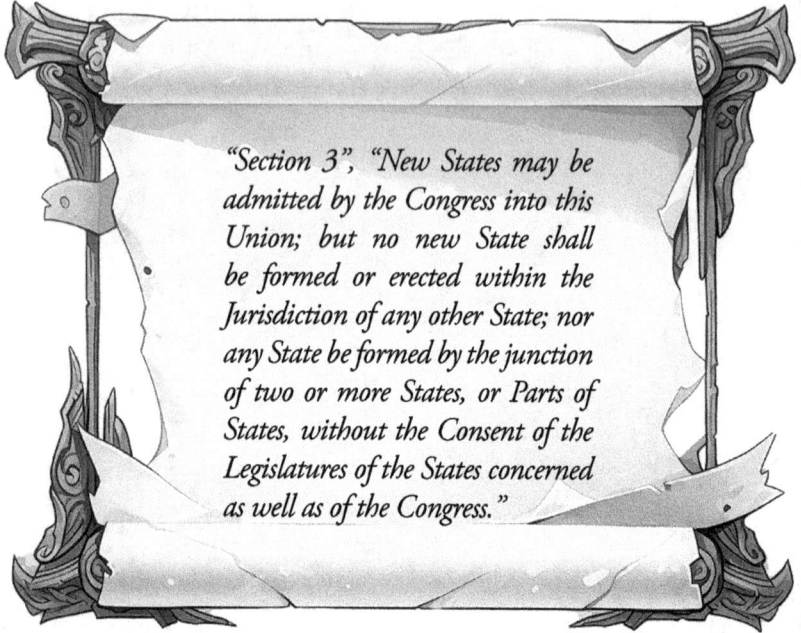

"Section 3", "New States may be admitted by the Congress into this Union; but no new State shall be formed or erected within the Jurisdiction of any other State; nor any State be formed by the junction of two or more States, or Parts of States, without the Consent of the Legislatures of the States concerned as well as of the Congress."

Congress has the power to admit new states, but any change in current states would have to be approved by that state's legislature in which that change would occur. Once again, it does not require a signature of the executive authority of that state. Time and time again, the governorship of any state is considered unimportant.

> *"The Congress shall have Power to dispose of and make all needful Rules and Regulations respecting the Territory or other Property belonging to the United States; and nothing in this Constitution shall be so construed as to Prejudice any Claims of the United States, or of any particular State."*

So here we give Congress the power to regulate the territories to which the United States holds.

> *"Section 4", "The United States shall guarantee to every State in this Union a Republican Form of Government, and shall protect each of them against Invasion; and on Application of the Legislature, or of the Executive (when the Legislature cannot be convened) against domestic violence."*

Here the United States guarantees a republican form of government to every State in the union and shall protect them from invasion or domestic violence when called on by the state's legislature, or governor only when the legislature cannot be convened.

"Article V", "The Congress whenever two thirds of both Houses shall deem it necessary, shall propose Amendments to this Constitution, or, on the Application of the Legislatures of two thirds of the several States, shall call a Convention for proposing Amendments, which in either Case, shall be valid to all Intents and Purposes, as Part of this Constitution, when ratified by the Legislatures of three fourths of the several States, or by Conventions in three fourths thereof, as the one or the other Mode of Ratification may be proposed by the Congress; provided that no Amendment which may be made prior to Year One thousand eight hundred and eight shall in any Manner affect the first and fourth Clauses in the Ninth Section of the first Article; and that no State, without its Consent, shall be deprived of its equal suffrage in the Senate."

Here we have two ways to amend the Constitution. The first requires two-thirds of both Houses of the legislature to propose amendments and have three-fourths of the States ratify them. The second is to have two-thirds of the States legislatures call for a convention for the purpose of proposing amendments, and it shall become part of the Constitution when three-fourths of the States ratify the changes. No state may deprive another state of its equality in the Senate. Either way, it's a high bar to get over. Some people theorize that this makes it a living, breathing document, that is having an ability to amend it, but it is not what is referred to with that Constitutional theory. This is simply a way to amend it. Here there is also a prohibition affecting the first and fourth clauses of the ninth section of Article I, prior to 1808. That time, however, has passed. It should be noted if the states were to call for a Constitutional Convention, everything would be up in the air much as it was when this document was worked on.

> "Article VI", "All Debts contracted and Engagements entered into, before the Adoption of this Constitution, shall be as valid against the United States under this Constitution, as under the Confederation."

This Constitution shall not change the owing of any debts or engagement previously owing to under The Articles of Confederation.

> "This Constitution, and the Laws of the United States which shall be made in Pursuance thereof; and all Treaties made, or which shall be made, under the Authority of the United States, shall be the supreme Law of the Land; and the Judges in every State shall be bound thereby, any Thing in the Constitution or Laws of any State to the Contrary notwithstanding."

Judges are bound by this Constitution and of the treaties made regardless of the laws of any state, and this constitution shall be the supreme law of the land.

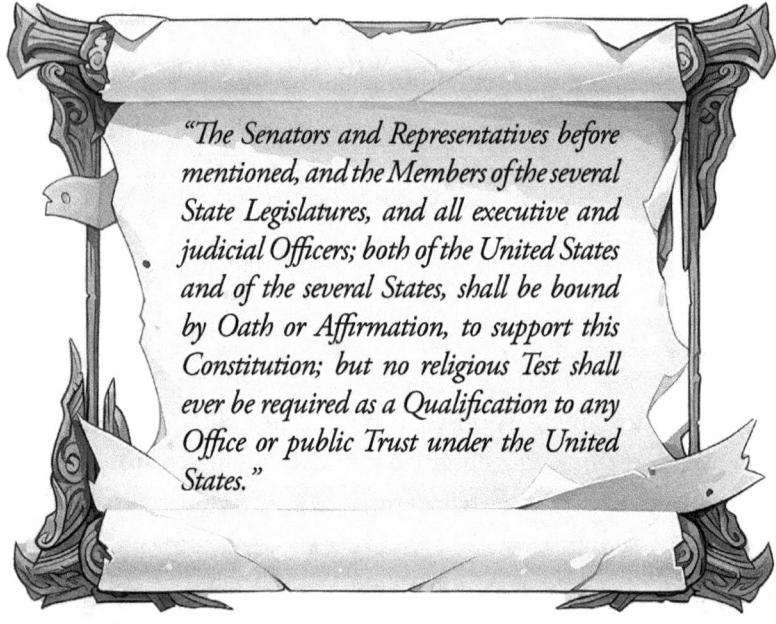

"The Senators and Representatives before mentioned, and the Members of the several State Legislatures, and all executive and judicial Officers; both of the United States and of the several States, shall be bound by Oath or Affirmation, to support this Constitution; but no religious Test shall ever be required as a Qualification to any Office or public Trust under the United States."

All elected officials are bound by oath or affirmation to support this Constitution, whether they be state or federal. It also guarantees there will be no religious test to hold any office or public trust.

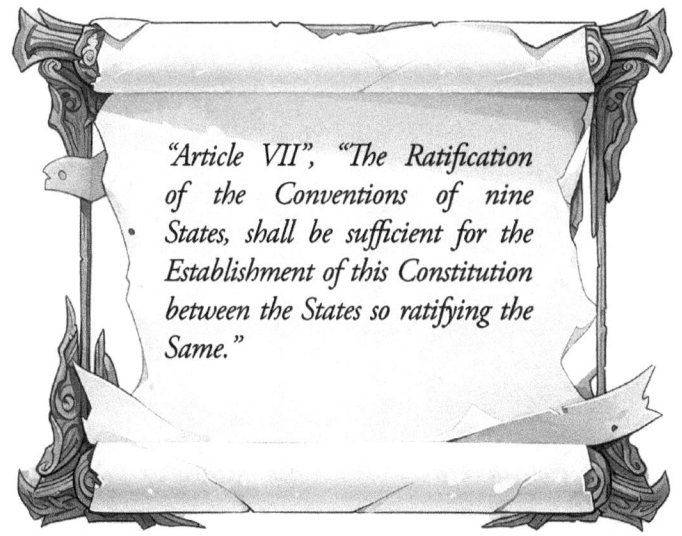

"*Article VII*", "*The Ratification of the Conventions of nine States, shall be sufficient for the Establishment of this Constitution between the States so ratifying the Same.*"

Here it says it will take nine states in conventions ratifying to establish the Constitution. This number is roughly three-fourths of all the States.

"*Done in Convention by the Unanimous Consent of the States present the Seventeenth Day of September in the Year of our Lord one thousand seven hundred and Eighty-seven and of the Independence of the United States of America the Twelfth In Witness whereof We have hereunto subscribed our Names,*"

Attest William Jackson
Secretary

Go; Washington-presidt.
And Deputy from Virginia
president

Delaware- Geo Reed
Gunning Bedford Junr.
John Dickinson
Richard Bassett
Jaco: Broom

New Hampshire-John Langdon
Nicholas Gilman

Massachusetts-National Gorham
Rufus King

Maryland- James McHenry
Dan of St Thos. Jenifer
Danl Carroll

Connecticut- Wm Saml. Johnson
Roger Shermann

Virginia-John Blair
James Madison Jr.

New York- Alexander Hamilton

North Carolina- Wm. Blount
Richd Dobbs Spraight
Hu Williamson

New Jersey - Wil Livingston
David Brearley
Wm. Patterson
Jona. Dayton

South Carolina- J. Rutledge
Charles Cotesworth Pinckney
Charles Pinckney
Pierce Butler

Pennsylvania- B. Franklin
Thomas Mifflin
Robt. Morris
Geo. Clymer
Thos. FitzSimons
Jared Ingersoll
James Wilson
Gouv. Morris

Georgia- William Few
Abr. Baldwin

Here are those that signed it. There were those who refused and fought ratification.

Our system is part federal and part national. We have established a nation and yet have maintained states' rights much as they would have in a federation of states. We have united ourselves for a common defense and to secure liberty and tranquility more than anything else.

I've heard it said that nobody cares about the Constitution, yet I have taken the oath a number of times. Our biggest problem is our elected officials themselves and the voters who don't know the Constitution, so they can't keep their feet to the fire. Our elected officials don't want to abide by it because the Constitution restricts government on a number of fronts. Politicians always want one thing, more Power.

The founders had a deep distrust of government and set up a system in which to deal with it, dividing up power at every turn. The founders knew the necessity of government but also the pitfalls. After all, they were self-governing in different ways throughout the colonies, so they compared what each state was doing like a self-government laboratory. I am well aware as I write this there will be people devoted to one party or another who will want to tear down anything I say, so I remind you of Washington's warning against political parties. Any group is only interested in their own preservation.

There are times in our republic where things herein have been violated. Our Constitution requires voluntary compliance or branches calling the others out on violations and the judiciary to intervene in cases of dispute. As we move forward, it must be said that judicial opinion is not always right. Bad law is just that, bad law, and judicial opinion can be corrupted like any other. That is why adherence to the Constitution is so important. Not adherence to the so-called settled law, which is sometimes not so settled!

With the end of the section containing the original constitution. I want to point out the language used. specifically noting their choice of what is capitalized because it gives you the idea of what they thought important as the language was written by the committee of style and arrangement in the constitutional convention. which they then voted on and adopted.

Before we get into the amendments, it should be discussed that a number of our founders were against a Bill of Rights, which are the first ten amendments. They started with twelve but only ten were adopted. One of the remainders was adopted 200 years later. That being the 27th amendment. Many of our founders felt it unnecessary because they were already in the language of the Constitution. Others thought they should be included with the Constitution. There was much debate about this in the convention hall. Later in the state ratifying conventions they had trouble getting the constitution ratified without a bill of rights which really drove this to be included. James Madison wrote up the Bill of Rights fulfilling a campaign promise, at the time he was running against James Monroe.

It was proposed during the first congress following ratification. So, they were adopted later. Eleven out of the twelve anyway.

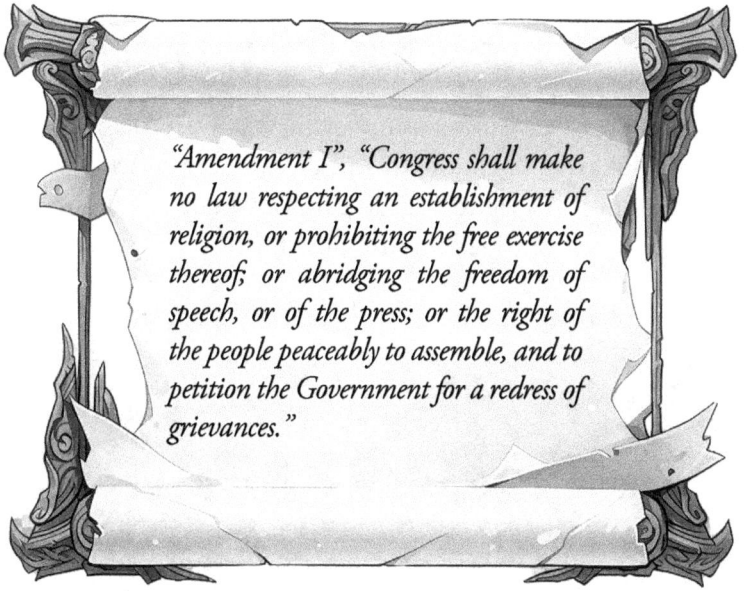

"Amendment I", "Congress shall make no law respecting an establishment of religion, or prohibiting the free exercise thereof; or abridging the freedom of speech, or of the press; or the right of the people peaceably to assemble, and to petition the Government for a redress of grievances."

The first amendment restricts Congress, not the states. It guarantees the freedom of religion, not from religion, and the freedom to worship as one see's fit. Government cannot govern anything in the confines of a church or other worship hall. You cannot violate a person's civil rights in the name of religion. It cannot curtail the freedom of speech or the press. People are allowed to speak freely and print whatever they choose, not in a free speech zone but anywhere, even to speech that may offend or repel others. It does not give people the freedom to slander or otherwise personally attack someone. You can basically say as you choose, so long as you do not hurt others. That's why you cannot yell Fire in a crowded theater, for instance; a statement often cited to limit free speech. It goes on to give the reason to petition the government for a redress of grievances, in other words, to seek change. The right of the people to peaceably assemble for this purpose. The right of assembly. Note the difference here between a freedom and a right. A right cannot be curtailed, but restrictions on freedoms are possible.

"Amendment II"," A well-regulated Militia, being necessary to the security of a free State, the right of the people to keep and bear Arms, shall not be infringed."

Here we have the right to keep and bear arms, and it shall not be infringed upon. This makes it an absolute right. It does not give it as a freedom. It also does not give it as a right to hunt or even self-defense. It is for a security of a free state. It comes from the understanding that you can't trust a standing army. Remember, there was a standing army here, quartered in people's homes, and taxes were levied to pay for this outrage against the colonists. It is here, the 2nd amendment, for the national defense period. It gives the reason that a well-regulated militia is necessary for a free state. So, what's a militia, I think the answer can be best found in Article VI of the Articles of Confederation where it states that "every state shall keep a well-regulated and disciplined militia, sufficiently armed and accounted, and shall provide and constantly have ready for use in public stores, a due number of field pieces and tents and a proper quantity of arms, ammunition and camp equipment." The purpose of requiring this is so it can be readily available to those with no weaponry themselves. Our founders understood the militia's well, as many of the founders served in them. What's important here is it's giving the right to the people, not a militia, army reserve or national guard unit. The purpose here is so the people can have ready in their homes, so that they can quickly get out to face whatever army or situation has made them called up. This right guarantees the others. You should note this is a right, not a freedom. Limitations cannot be instituted without surrendering other rights.

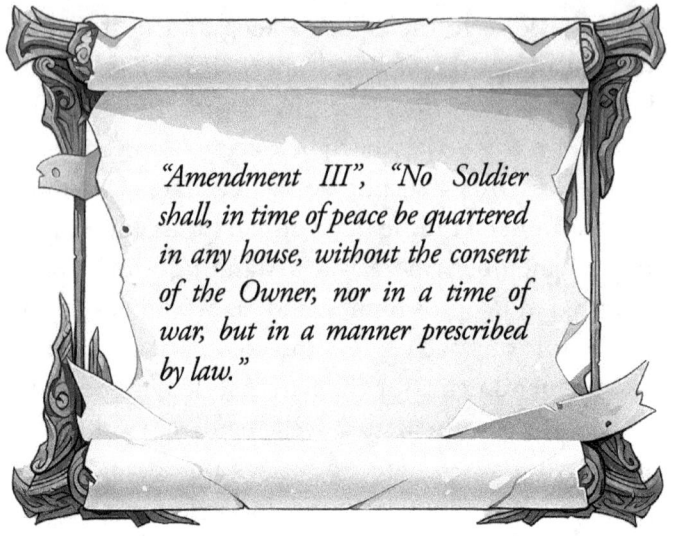

"Amendment III", "No Soldier shall, in time of peace be quartered in any house, without the consent of the Owner, nor in a time of war, but in a manner prescribed by law."

This comes right out of the experience of the war for independence, where housing or quartering soldiers is exactly what the British did. No person shall be forced to house armed forces during a time of peace without the homeowner's approval or in a time of war unless in a manner prescribed by Law. This amendment was considered by our founders to be one of the most important if not the most important amendment.

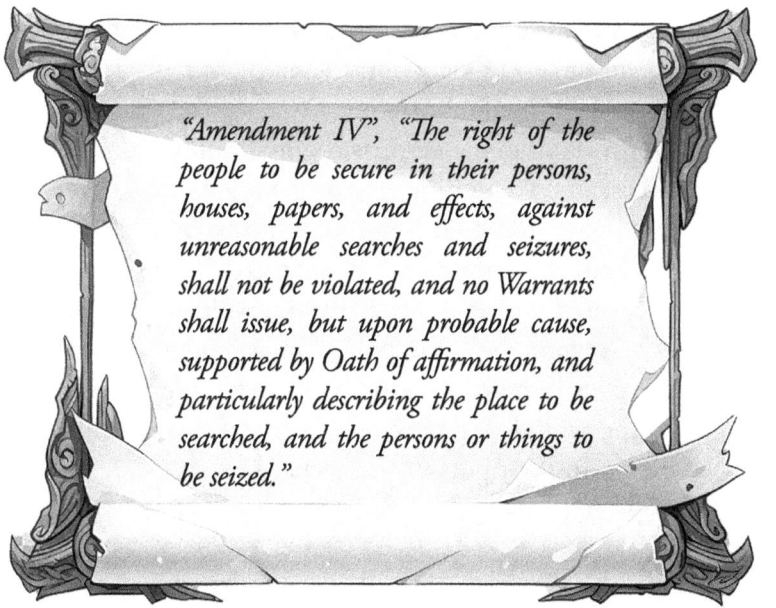

"Amendment IV", "The right of the people to be secure in their persons, houses, papers, and effects, against unreasonable searches and seizures, shall not be violated, and no Warrants shall issue, but upon probable cause, supported by Oath of affirmation, and particularly describing the place to be searched, and the persons or things to be seized."

The right of the people to be free and secure in their homes, persons, papers, and effects. Effectively no one can be searched or have their property searched without a due course of law. There must be probable cause for any search, and a reasonable belief that some law has been violated supported by oath or affirmation. Meaning you must have statements from individuals with some knowledge or belief that a crime has been committed and that they have seen or otherwise have knowledge of possession. A warrant must be specific in such ways as to places to be searched and specifics of what or whom should be seized. So, you can't have an open-ended warrant. This security, however, does not institute a perceived right to privacy. Information in a public domain negates secure items, ideas, etc. However, in the use of some public platform or private companies' platform, it is no longer considered private property because you made it public. You don't own the platform. If you give permission for an officer of the law to search something, it's over because you gave up the right to search a home or trunk of a car. If it's locked, they must have a warrant. If something is discovered during a search, as long as it was a legal search, it would be admissible. I am getting too deep in the weeds here. An open-ended warrant to do anything would not be valid Constitutionally. This all gets into the rights of the accused.

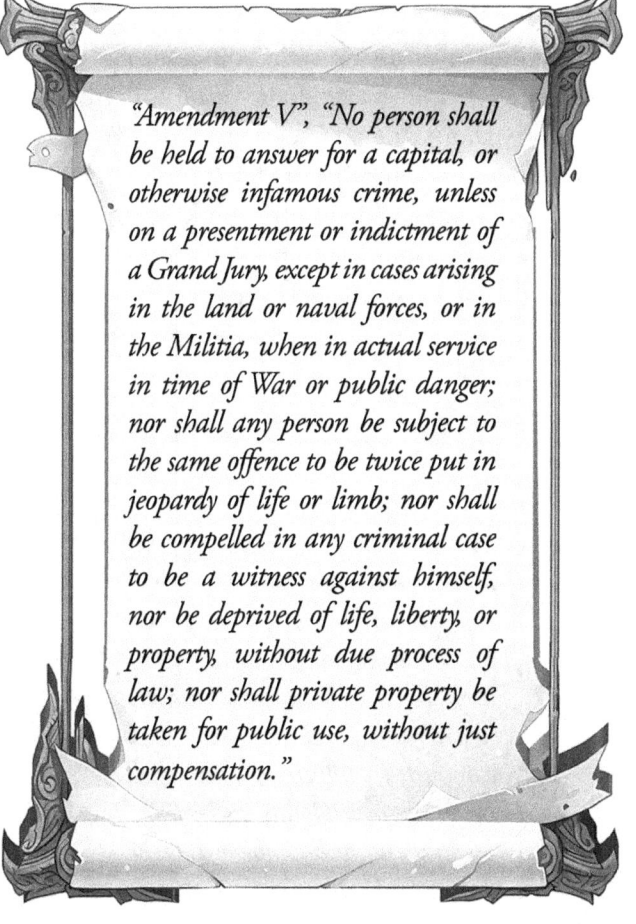

"Amendment V", "No person shall be held to answer for a capital, or otherwise infamous crime, unless on a presentment or indictment of a Grand Jury, except in cases arising in the land or naval forces, or in the Militia, when in actual service in time of War or public danger; nor shall any person be subject to the same offence to be twice put in jeopardy of life or limb; nor shall be compelled in any criminal case to be a witness against himself, nor be deprived of life, liberty, or property, without due process of law; nor shall private property be taken for public use, without just compensation."

To be held to answer for an infamous crime, one must be presented with proper charges arising from a grand jury, with the exception of armed forces when in service during a time of war or public danger. No person can be tried twice for the same offense. In other words, double jeopardy. One cannot be forced to be a witness against oneself. One has the right to remain silent. If you take to the witness stand in your own defense for instance, then you have given up that right and in that case, you can then be cross examined. No one can be deprived of life, liberty, or property without due course of law. You cannot have your property taken without fair reimbursement in the event it is taken for public good. This is not if it is taken due to violations of law. In essence, this is more of the rights of the accused.

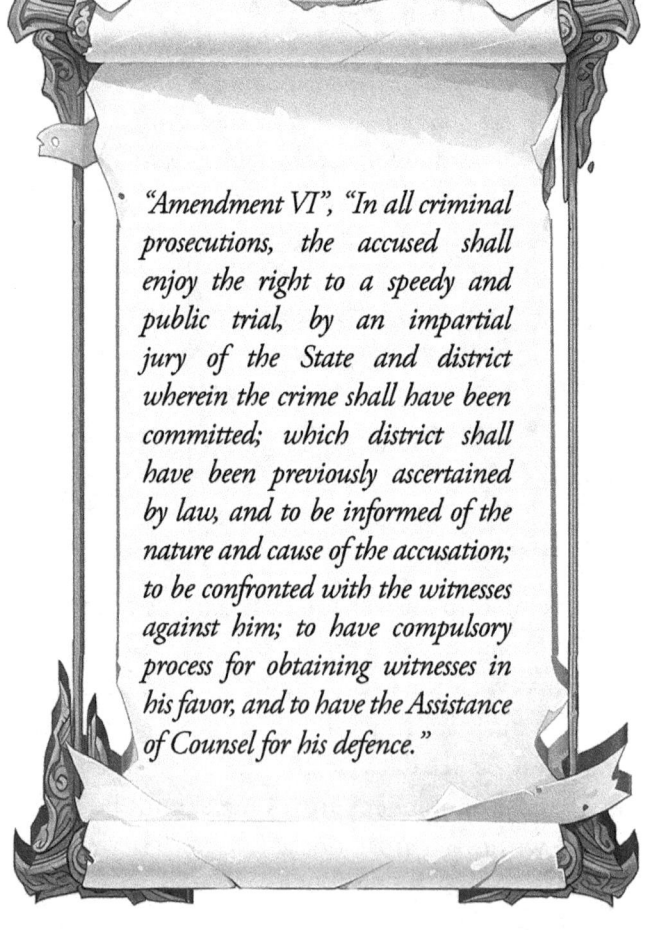

"Amendment VI", "In all criminal prosecutions, the accused shall enjoy the right to a speedy and public trial, by an impartial jury of the State and district wherein the crime shall have been committed; which district shall have been previously ascertained by law, and to be informed of the nature and cause of the accusation; to be confronted with the witnesses against him; to have compulsory process for obtaining witnesses in his favor, and to have the Assistance of Counsel for his defence."

Each person in the event of a criminal prosecution shall have the right to a speedy trial by an impartial jury in the area where the crime was committed. Trials cannot drag on for years and years. There are times when a trial cannot be held in the immediate area due to the inability of a fair jury. In these cases, the trial may be moved after being asked by the defense. You have the right to be informed of the alleged crimes against you, have the right to obtain witnesses in your defense, and have the benefit of council. We are spelling out the rights of the accused here, showing what should happen for trial.

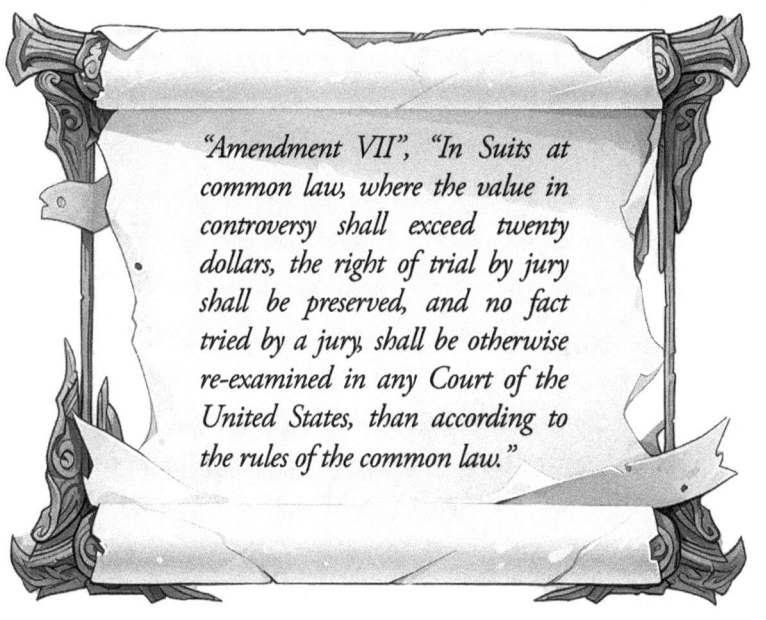

"Amendment VII", "In Suits at common law, where the value in controversy shall exceed twenty dollars, the right of trial by jury shall be preserved, and no fact tried by a jury, shall be otherwise re-examined in any Court of the United States, than according to the rules of the common law."

In any common law case where the value exceeds $20.00, a right to trial by jury shall be intact. And no one can be later tried or have the same offense re-examined. In other words, you cannot be tried twice for the same offense, otherwise known as double jeopardy. Although this only applies to common lawsuits. You cannot be tried in common law and later be tried in federal court for the same act.

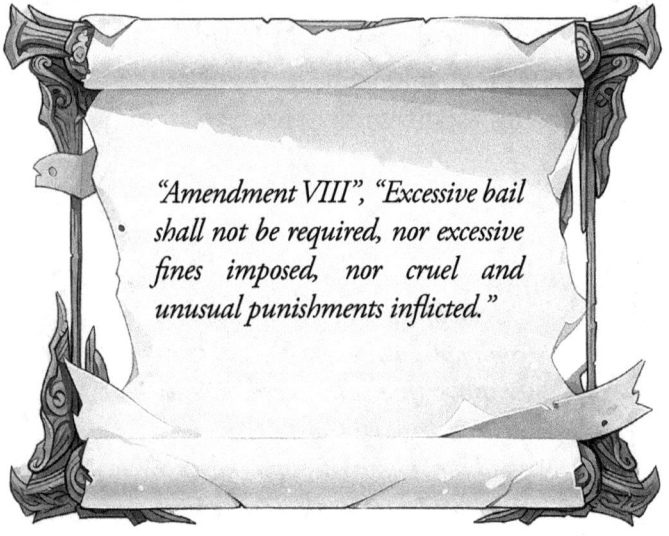

"Amendment VIII", "Excessive bail shall not be required, nor excessive fines imposed, nor cruel and unusual punishments inflicted."

You cannot impose bails so high that one cannot possibly pay, or fines so excessive, or any punishment so cruel in nature that it would negate some sense of justice.

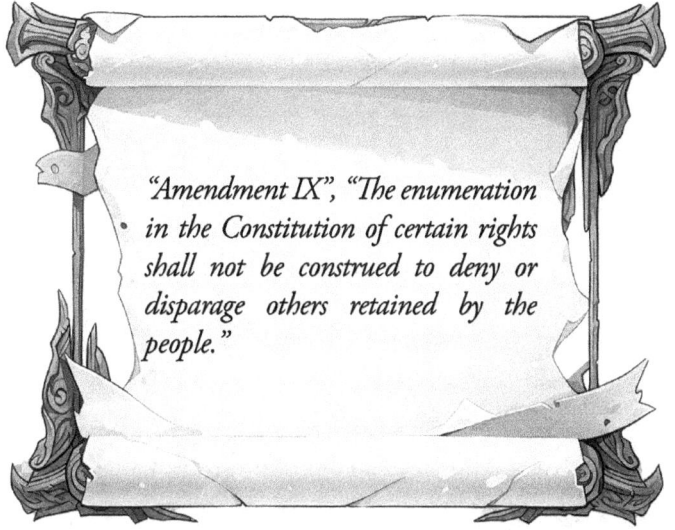

"Amendment IX", "The enumeration in the Constitution of certain rights shall not be construed to deny or disparage others retained by the people."

In so numbering these rights, the Bill of Rights does not take away any natural rights the people hold. So, in essence it tells us there are rights not spelled out. Our founders believed in natural rights, those given by God almighty, or natures law. For instance, the right to move between states, choose your own occupation, your spouse or even whether to marry or who to leave your money too through the writing of a will, or even that of self-defense. Many of these things should be obvious which is why most people don't understand the concept. Many were opposed to a Bill of Rights because they believed to have already spelled them out throughout the Constitution itself. James Madison wrote up the bill of rights taking the complaints during the ratifying conventions. Something he'd promised while running for a seat in the house of representatives, against James Monroe.

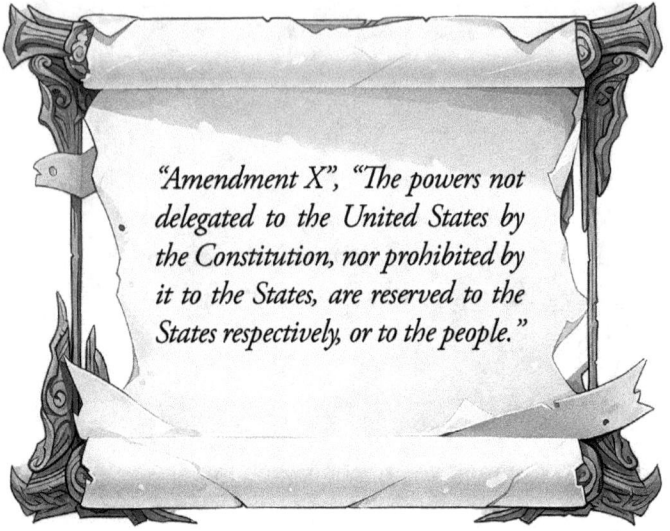

"Amendment X", "The powers not delegated to the United States by the Constitution, nor prohibited by it to the States, are reserved to the States respectively, or to the people."

Here is a catch-all phrase if I've ever seen one. The Constitution is a document encompassing the rights and duties given to the federal government by the states in convention and restricting others so as to reserve them for the states. So, if it's not given herein to the federal government, nor restricted by it to the states, then the rights are reserved by the states and the people. Everything is not the duty of the federal government. The federal government is only given certain powers necessary to run a National or federal government and nothing else.

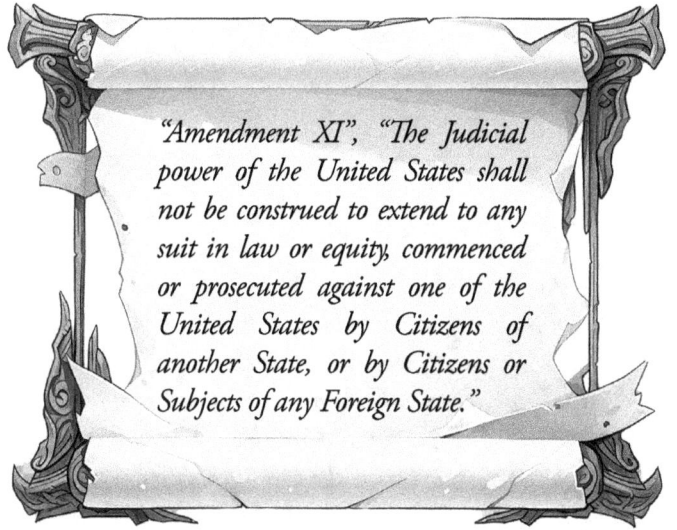

"Amendment XI", "The Judicial power of the United States shall not be construed to extend to any suit in law or equity, commenced or prosecuted against one of the United States by Citizens of another State, or by Citizens or Subjects of any Foreign State."

In other words, the federal judiciary has no standing to interfere with lawsuits arising from a citizen of one state suing the other state, nor does any foreigner have a legal right to sue the United States in our federal courts. This amendment is here due to a supreme court decision Chisholm vs. Georgia. After Georgia lost the case Congress sent this amendment in hopes no such case would again come before the high court.

"Amendment XII", "The Electors shall meet in their respective states, and vote by ballot for President and Vice-President, one of whom, at least, shall not be an inhabitant of the same state with themselves; they shall name in their ballots the person voted for as President, and in distinct ballots the person voted for as Vice President, and they shall make distinct lists of all persons voted for as President, and of all persons voted for as Vice President, and of the number of votes for each, which lists they shall sign and certify, and transmit sealed to the seat of the government of the United States, directed to the President of the Senate;- The President of the Senate shall, in the presence of the Senate and House of Representatives, open all the certificates and the votes shall then be counted,— The person having the greatest

number of votes for President, shall be the President, if such number be a majority of the whole number of Electors appointed; and if no person have such majority, then from the persons having the highest numbers not exceeding three on the list of those voted for as President, the House of Representatives shall choose immediately, by ballot, the President. But in choosing the President, the votes shall be taken by states, the representation from each state having one vote; a quorum for this purpose shall consist of a member or members from two-thirds of the states, and a majority of all the states shall be necessary to a choice. And if the House of Representatives shall not choose a President whenever the right of choice shall devolve upon them, before the fourth day of March next following, then the Vice-President shall act as President, as in the case of the death or other constitutional disability of the President—The person having the greatest number of votes as Vice-President, shall be the Vice President, if such number be a majority of the whole number of Electors appointed, and if no person have a majority, then from the two highest numbers on the list, the Senate shall choose the Vice-President;

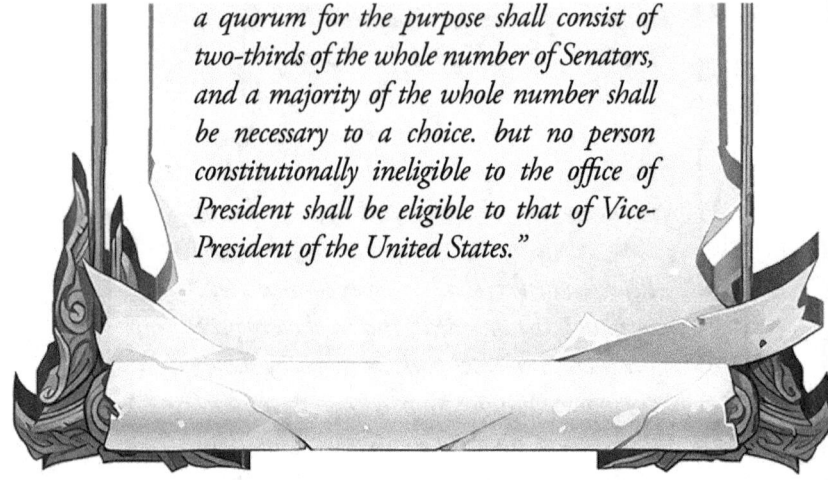

a quorum for the purpose shall consist of two-thirds of the whole number of Senators, and a majority of the whole number shall be necessary to a choice. but no person constitutionally ineligible to the office of President shall be eligible to that of Vice-President of the United States."

Much of Article II Section I is replaced here by amendment. Basically, it is cleaned up to make it more precise. This deals with the electoral college. The differences include that the vice president and president vote shall be distinct as they shall state who shall be president and who shall be vice president. Thus, it ends the problem of a president of one party and a vice president of another. Once all ballots are opened by the president of the Senate during a joint session of Congress for such purposes, if the count is tied, then the House of Representatives shall choose from the top three to be the President. Voting by state, each state has one vote. The Senate shall choose the vice president, with each senator having one vote. The choice is from the top two on the list. Again, only if tied. If there is no one chosen by March 4th, then the vice president shall act as president, the same as if the president had died or been removed by disability. See Article II Section 1.

In 1796 John Adams was elected President and Thomas Jefferson Vice president this is the only time that a President was of one party and the vice President was another, Adams a Federalist and Jefferson a Republican. Which is why this was changed and why we now have Presidential running mates.

The XIII – XVth amendments are called reconstruction amendments. Following the emancipation proclamation, and the Lincoln assassination, amendments were passed to take into count the civil war and to give the former slaves rights under the law.

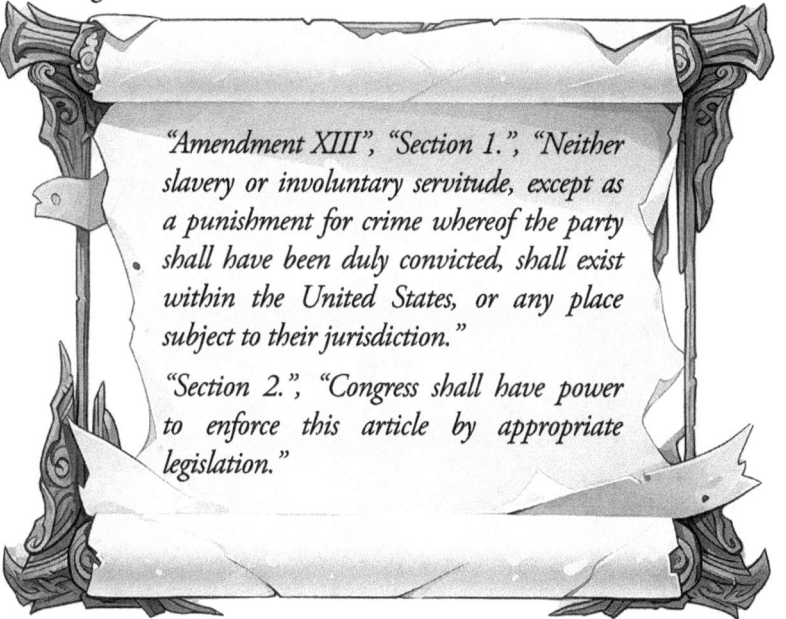

"Amendment XIII", "Section 1.", "Neither slavery or involuntary servitude, except as a punishment for crime whereof the party shall have been duly convicted, shall exist within the United States, or any place subject to their jurisdiction."

"Section 2.", "Congress shall have power to enforce this article by appropriate legislation."

Here we have the beginning of amendments dealing with the emancipation of the slaves. It makes both slavery and involuntary servitude, other than for the punishment of a crime, illegal. This had been a compromise, slavery, that is. The convention had been worried about Georgia and South Carolina specifically not accepting the Constitution without it.

Section 2 this is the first place where it gives Congress the power of enforcement through legislation. This becomes a routine practice afterwards.

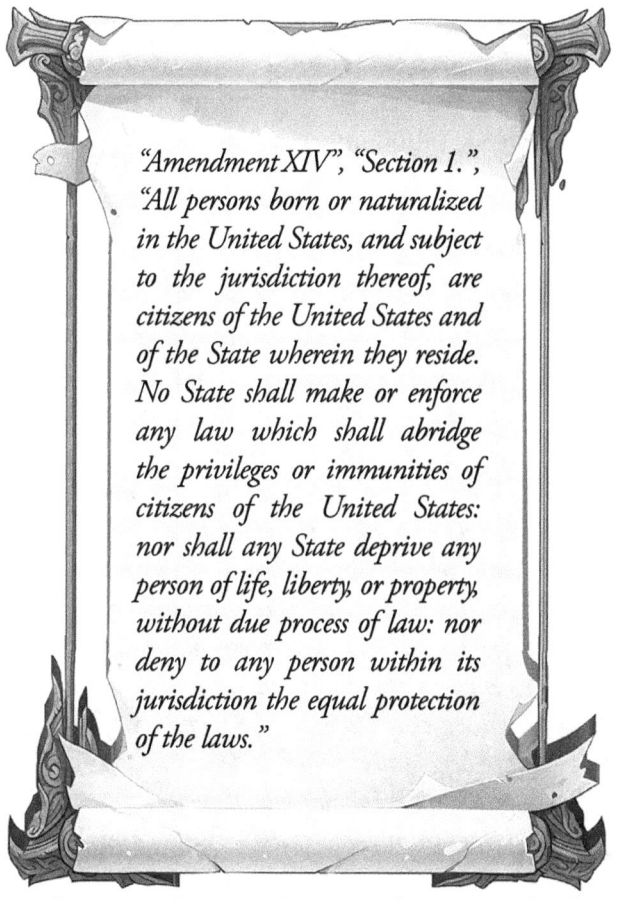

"Amendment XIV", "Section 1.", "All persons born or naturalized in the United States, and subject to the jurisdiction thereof, are citizens of the United States and of the State wherein they reside. No State shall make or enforce any law which shall abridge the privileges or immunities of citizens of the United States: nor shall any State deprive any person of life, liberty, or property, without due process of law: nor deny to any person within its jurisdiction the equal protection of the laws."

All persons born in the United States and subject to its jurisdiction are made a citizen of the United States. This makes all the former slaves and their children and those born during indentured servitude citizens of the United States, and citizens of the state in which they live. This does not give foreign-born individuals or their offspring citizenship, as they are not subject to our jurisdictions. It also forbids states from taking privileges and immunities from their citizens. Guarantees all citizens of any state equal protection under the color of law. It also forbids any state from taking life, liberty, or property from anyone without due process of law.

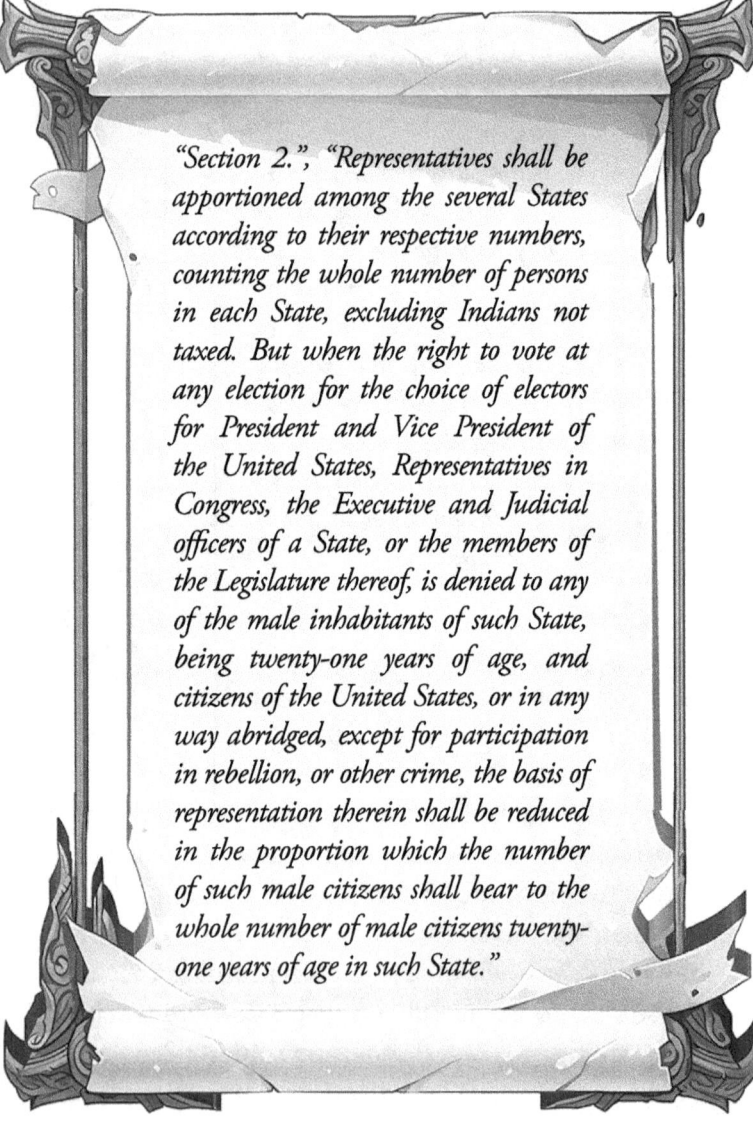

"Section 2.", "Representatives shall be apportioned among the several States according to their respective numbers, counting the whole number of persons in each State, excluding Indians not taxed. But when the right to vote at any election for the choice of electors for President and Vice President of the United States, Representatives in Congress, the Executive and Judicial officers of a State, or the members of the Legislature thereof, is denied to any of the male inhabitants of such State, being twenty-one years of age, and citizens of the United States, or in any way abridged, except for participation in rebellion, or other crime, the basis of representation therein shall be reduced in the proportion which the number of such male citizens shall bear to the whole number of male citizens twenty-one years of age in such State."

Representatives shall be apportioned throughout the several states by the numbers counting all persons except Indians not taxed. No males shall be denied the right to vote, spelling out all the federal and state offices, except for participation in crimes and rebellion. Representatives in the state shall be reduced by the number denied. Here we are clearly punishing the southern states and the citizens who fought in the rebellion for the Confederate States of America. This also updates Article I Section 2, which has the Three-Fifths Clause for counting citizens for apportionment, which hereby is eliminated.

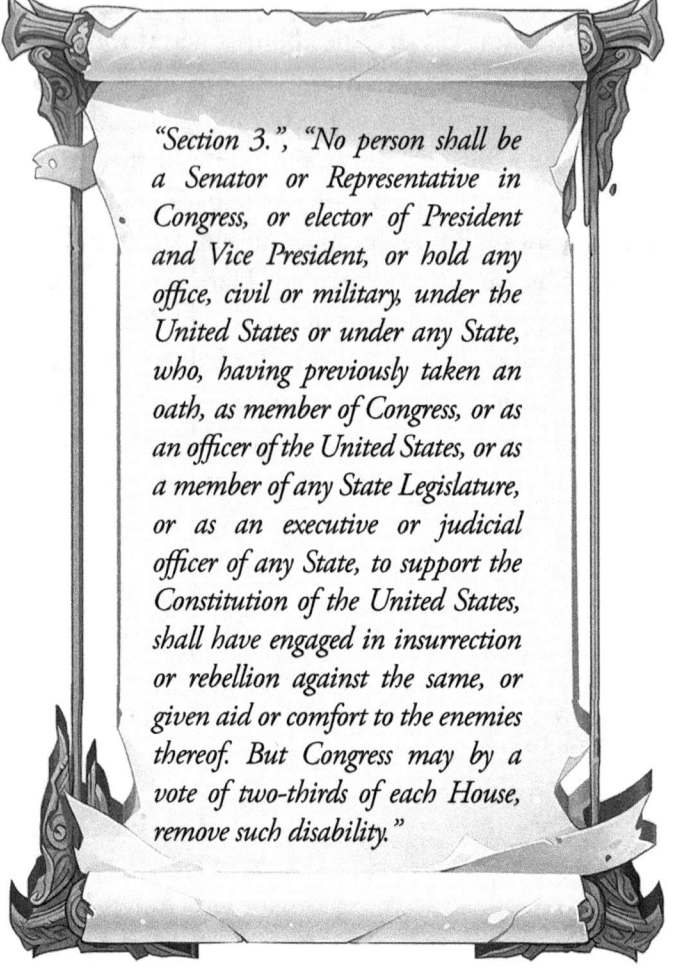

"Section 3.", "No person shall be a Senator or Representative in Congress, or elector of President and Vice President, or hold any office, civil or military, under the United States or under any State, who, having previously taken an oath, as member of Congress, or as an officer of the United States, or as a member of any State Legislature, or as an executive or judicial officer of any State, to support the Constitution of the United States, shall have engaged in insurrection or rebellion against the same, or given aid or comfort to the enemies thereof. But Congress may by a vote of two-thirds of each House, remove such disability."

I must wonder here, if Lincoln would have lived, what he would have thought about this "Malice towards none." Basically, all persons elected to any office, because all officers do take an oath to support and defend the Constitution of the United States, are hereby denied the ability to hold any office due to supporting the Confederacy. We are clearly punishing the southern states here and their leaders. But to the victor go the spoils!

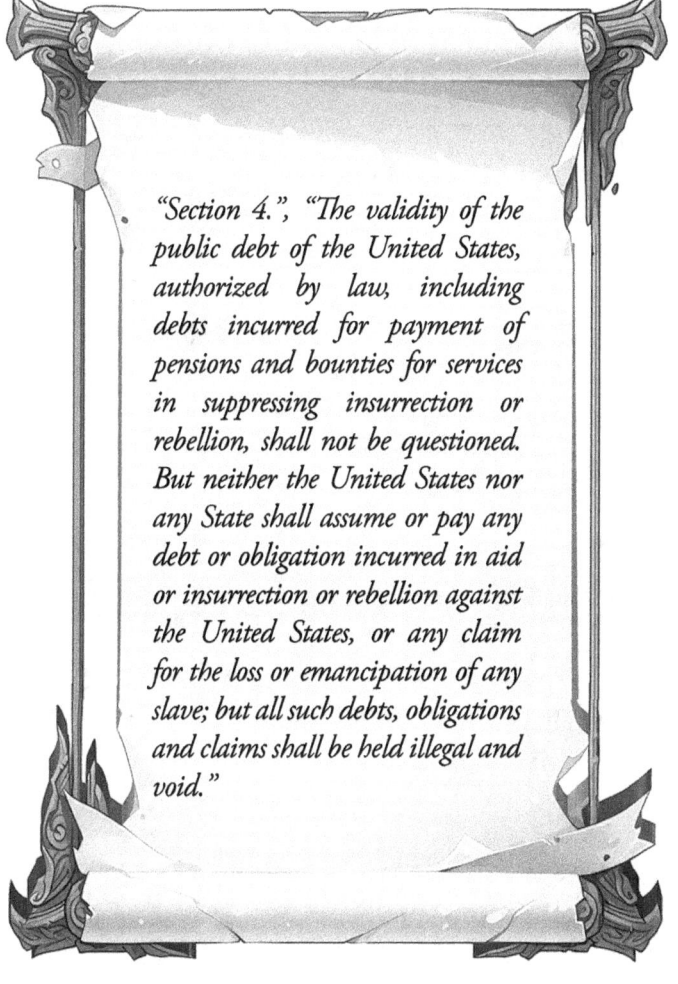

"Section 4.", "The validity of the public debt of the United States, authorized by law, including debts incurred for payment of pensions and bounties for services in suppressing insurrection or rebellion, shall not be questioned. But neither the United States nor any State shall assume or pay any debt or obligation incurred in aid or insurrection or rebellion against the United States, or any claim for the loss or emancipation of any slave; but all such debts, obligations and claims shall be held illegal and void."

All debts the federal government may owe due to suppressing the rebellion of the southern states shall not be questioned, what they're talking about here is items confiscated by the northern army in the course of fighting the war such as horses, cattle really anything of this nature. All debts due to the Civil War by the southern states shall be null and void, and no claims against the United States for the freeing of slaves shall be held legitimate.

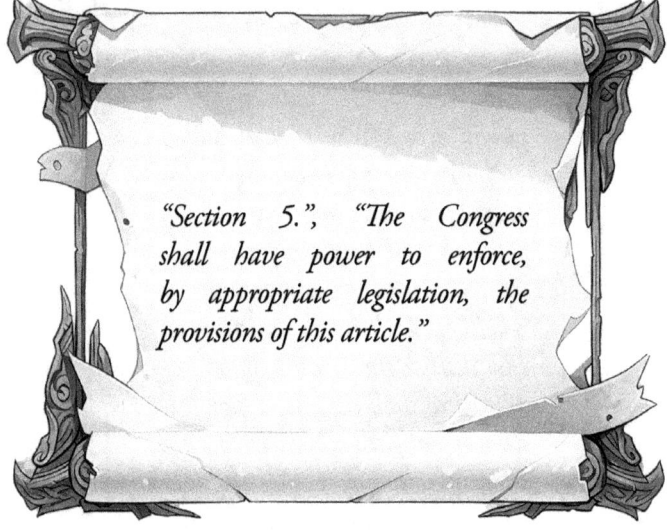

"Section 5.", "The Congress shall have power to enforce, by appropriate legislation, the provisions of this article."

Here again, we have Congress given the right to enforcement through legislation.

"Amendment XV", "Section 1.", "The right of citizens of the United States to vote shall not be denied or abridged by the United States or by any State on account of race, color, or previous condition of servitude."

"Section 2", "The Congress shall have power to enforce the article by appropriate legislation."

Here we are given the right to vote. We will no longer exclude voting based on race, color, or anyone held in slavery or involuntary servitude. This ends the section dealing with the late Civil War and gives absolute freedom and equality under the law to all citizens held in slavery or involuntary servitude.

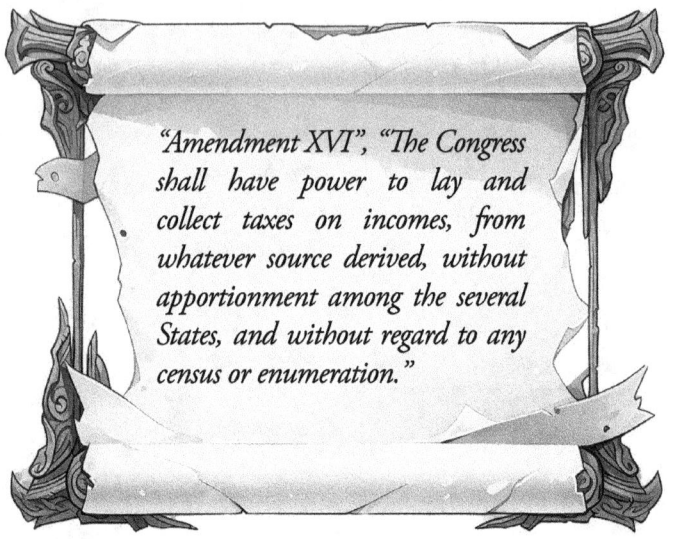

"Amendment XVI", "The Congress shall have power to lay and collect taxes on incomes, from whatever source derived, without apportionment among the several States, and without regard to any census or enumeration."

This gives Congress the right to collect income tax. Income tax was first established to pay for Civil War expenses.

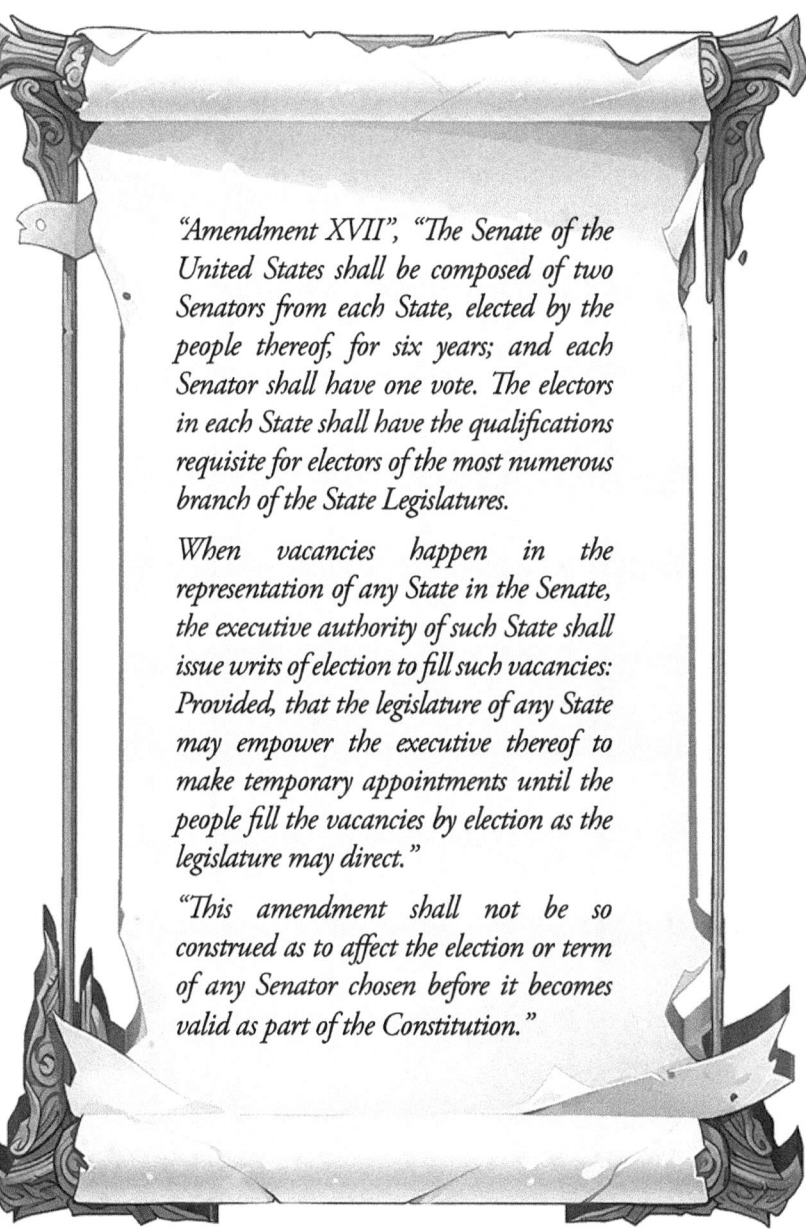

"Amendment XVII", "The Senate of the United States shall be composed of two Senators from each State, elected by the people thereof, for six years; and each Senator shall have one vote. The electors in each State shall have the qualifications requisite for electors of the most numerous branch of the State Legislatures.

When vacancies happen in the representation of any State in the Senate, the executive authority of such State shall issue writs of election to fill such vacancies: Provided, that the legislature of any State may empower the executive thereof to make temporary appointments until the people fill the vacancies by election as the legislature may direct."

"This amendment shall not be so construed as to affect the election or term of any Senator chosen before it becomes valid as part of the Constitution."

This replaces sections of Article I Section 3. To provide for an election by the people for the Senate rather than having them chosen by the legislature of that state. The intent is that the senate is to represent the states and the house represent the people which is why the equal suffrage of the senate cannot be changed by amendment.

"Amendment XVIII", "Section 1" *After one year from the ratification of this article the manufacture, sale, or transportation of intoxicating liquors within, the importation thereof into, or the exportation thereof from the United States and all territory subject to the jurisdiction thereof for beverage purposes is hereby prohibited."*

"Section 2.", "The Congress and the several States shall have concurrent power to enforce this article by appropriate legislation."

"Section 3". "This article shall be inoperative unless it shall have been ratified as an amendment to the Constitution by the legislatures of the several States, as provided in the Constitution within seven years from the date of the submission hereof to the States by the Congress."

Here we have prohibition, which is later repealed. See the 21st amendment. Basically no one can sell, import, or export any intoxicating liquors within the jurisdiction of the United States and its territory. There had been a very large prohibition movement in the country. The results of this were a burgeoning mob, organized crime, gang warfare, and complete disrespect for the law. It really was a complete failure. People made gin in their bathtubs. The other interesting thing here is it's the first time an amendment was sent to the states with a time limit for ratification.

"Amendment XIX", "*The right of the citizens of the United States to vote shall not be denied or abridged by the United States or by any State on account of sex.*

Congress shall have power to enforce this article by appropriate legislation."

This gives women the right to vote. There was a great political movement for both these last two amendments called women's suffrage.

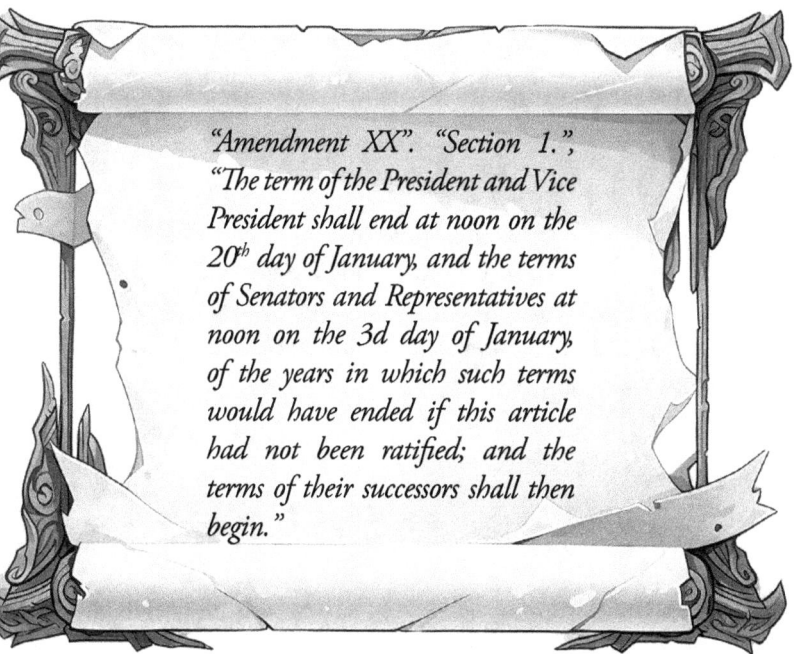

"Amendment XX". "Section 1.", "The term of the President and Vice President shall end at noon on the 20th day of January, and the terms of Senators and Representatives at noon on the 3d day of January, of the years in which such terms would have ended if this article had not been ratified; and the terms of their successors shall then begin."

This changes the beginning and end of the president's and his vice president's term from March 4th to January 20th and establishes when the congressional term shall begin. This shortens the time between elections and when the President shall take office.

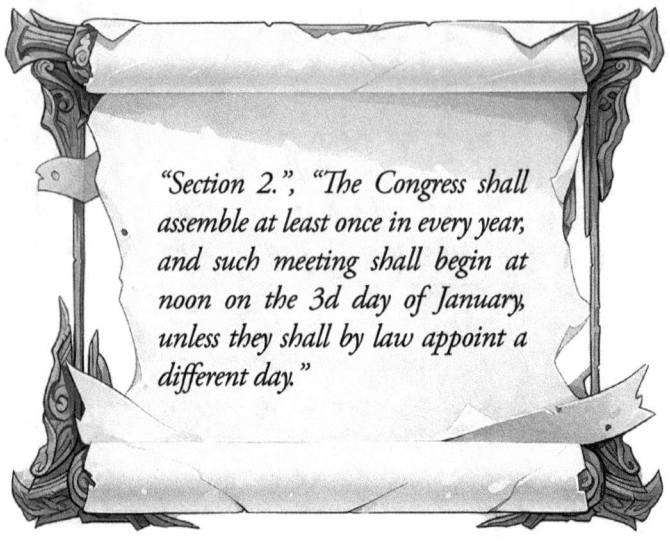

"Section 2.", "The Congress shall assemble at least once in every year, and such meeting shall begin at noon on the 3d day of January, unless they shall by law appoint a different day."

This changes Article I Section 4, which is the date when Congress shall meet from the first Monday in December to the 3rd of January.

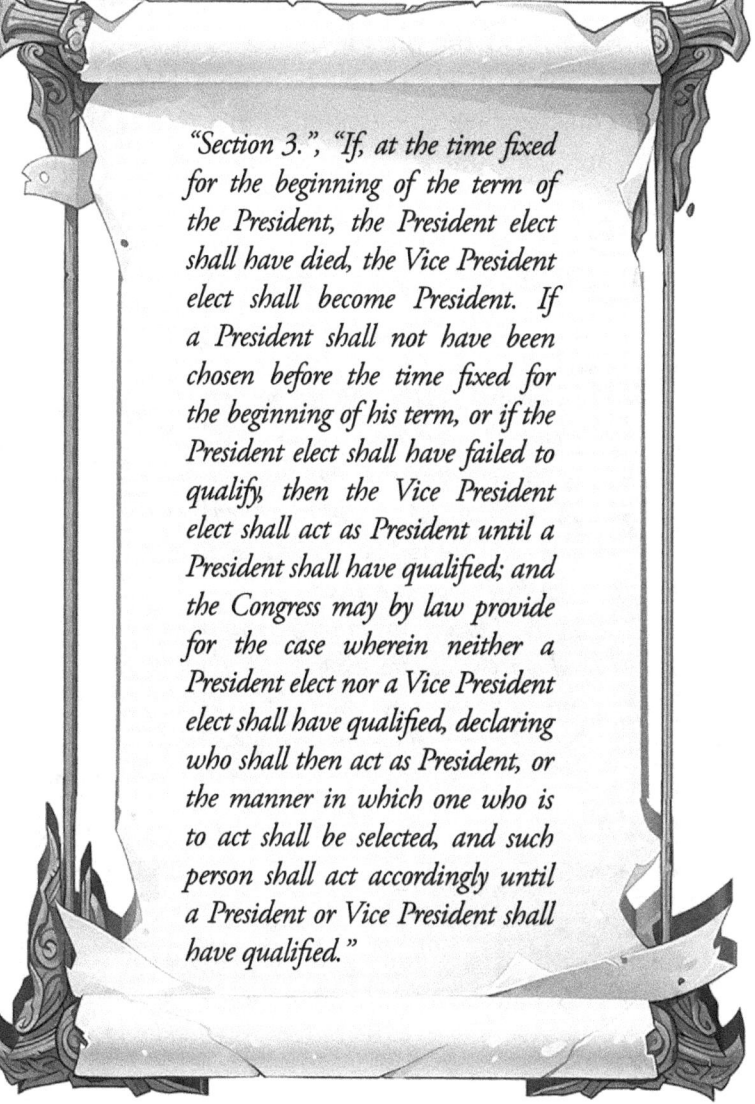

"Section 3.", "If, at the time fixed for the beginning of the term of the President, the President elect shall have died, the Vice President elect shall become President. If a President shall not have been chosen before the time fixed for the beginning of his term, or if the President elect shall have failed to qualify, then the Vice President elect shall act as President until a President shall have qualified; and the Congress may by law provide for the case wherein neither a President elect nor a Vice President elect shall have qualified, declaring who shall then act as President, or the manner in which one who is to act shall be selected, and such person shall act accordingly until a President or Vice President shall have qualified."

This has to do with the succession of power. If a president has not been chosen at the beginning of a new term or if the president-elect has died, then the vice president-elect shall become president. If neither qualify, then Congress shall choose who shall act as president until a president or vice president has qualified.

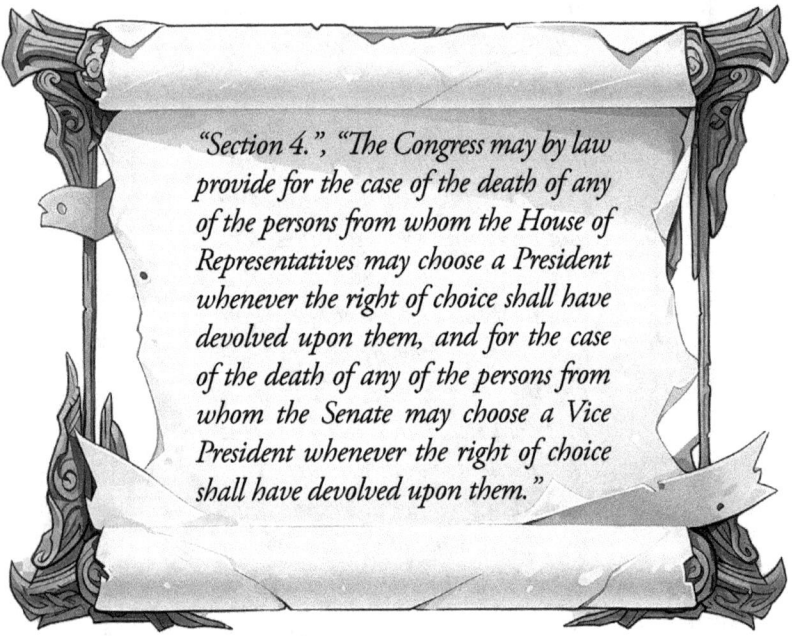

"Section 4.", "The Congress may by law provide for the case of the death of any of the persons from whom the House of Representatives may choose a President whenever the right of choice shall have devolved upon them, and for the case of the death of any of the persons from whom the Senate may choose a Vice President whenever the right of choice shall have devolved upon them."

Congress may by law provide for the case in which death occurs among those with which the House or Senate may make their choice.

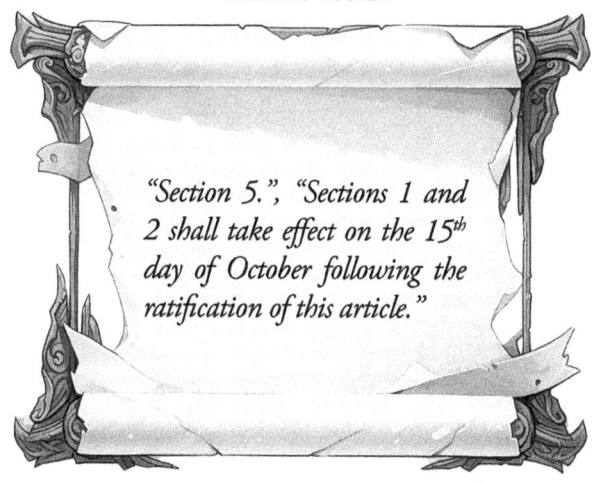

"Section 5.", "Sections 1 and 2 shall take effect on the 15th day of October following the ratification of this article."

Simply put, this just sets a date for when sections 1 and 2 shall begin.

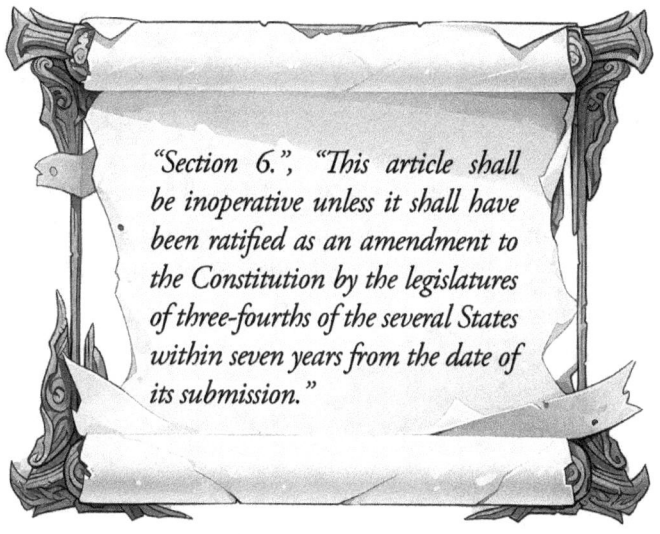

"Section 6.", "This article shall be inoperative unless it shall have been ratified as an amendment to the Constitution by the legislatures of three-fourths of the several States within seven years from the date of its submission."

Here again, we have put a time limit on the passage of this amendment, and it reaffirms the procedure in which the constitution shall be amended.

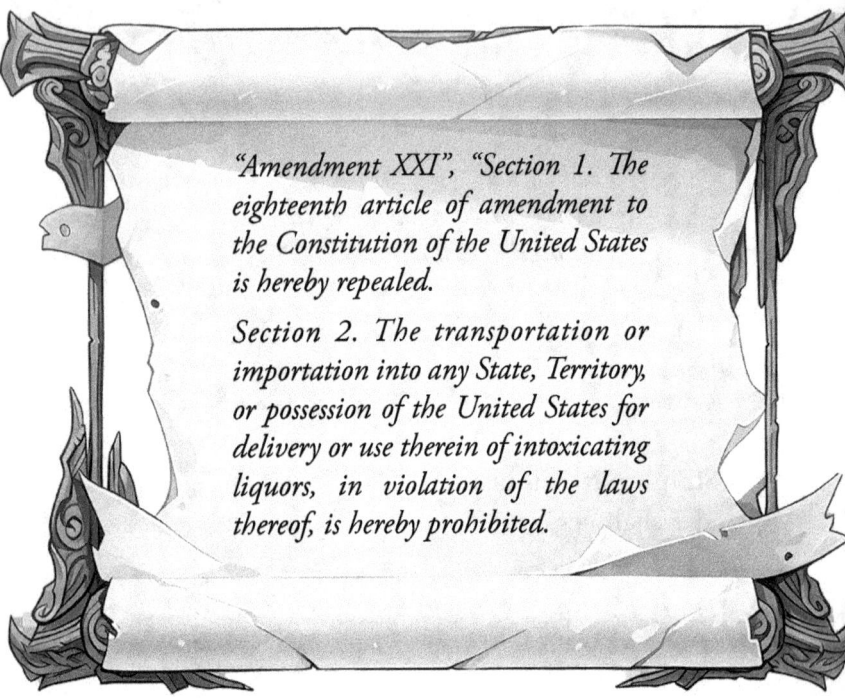

"*Amendment XXI*", "*Section 1. The eighteenth article of amendment to the Constitution of the United States is hereby repealed.*

Section 2. The transportation or importation into any State, Territory, or possession of the United States for delivery or use therein of intoxicating liquors, in violation of the laws thereof, is hereby prohibited."

Herein is a complete repeal of the 18th amendment to the Constitution. See the 18th amendment. This repeals prohibition! The prohibition of alcohol led to a rise in organized crime and mob violence. It was an abstract failure.

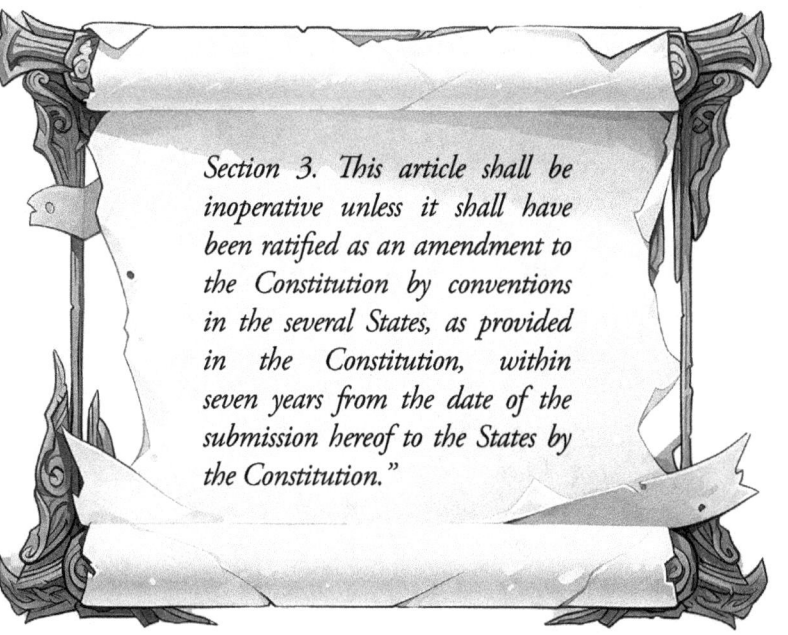

Section 3. This article shall be inoperative unless it shall have been ratified as an amendment to the Constitution by conventions in the several States, as provided in the Constitution, within seven years from the date of the submission hereof to the States by the Constitution."

The interesting thing here in section three is it is the only time an amendment was ratified by a convention of states.

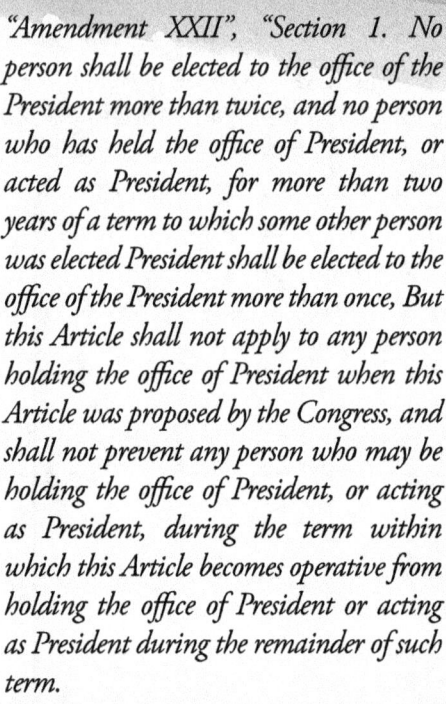

"Amendment XXII", "Section 1. No person shall be elected to the office of the President more than twice, and no person who has held the office of President, or acted as President, for more than two years of a term to which some other person was elected President shall be elected to the office of the President more than once, But this Article shall not apply to any person holding the office of President when this Article was proposed by the Congress, and shall not prevent any person who may be holding the office of President, or acting as President, during the term within which this Article becomes operative from holding the office of President or acting as President during the remainder of such term.

Section 2. This article shall be inoperative unless it shall have been ratified as an amendment to the Constitution by the legislatures of three-fourths of the several States within seven years from the date of its submission to the States by the Congress".

Basically, here we are restricting anyone from being president longer than two terms. This is a response to the four terms Franklin D. Roosevelt served as president. This was changed due to the power of incumbency. It was a tradition started by President Washington to only serve two terms, here it is placed in Constitutional hands.

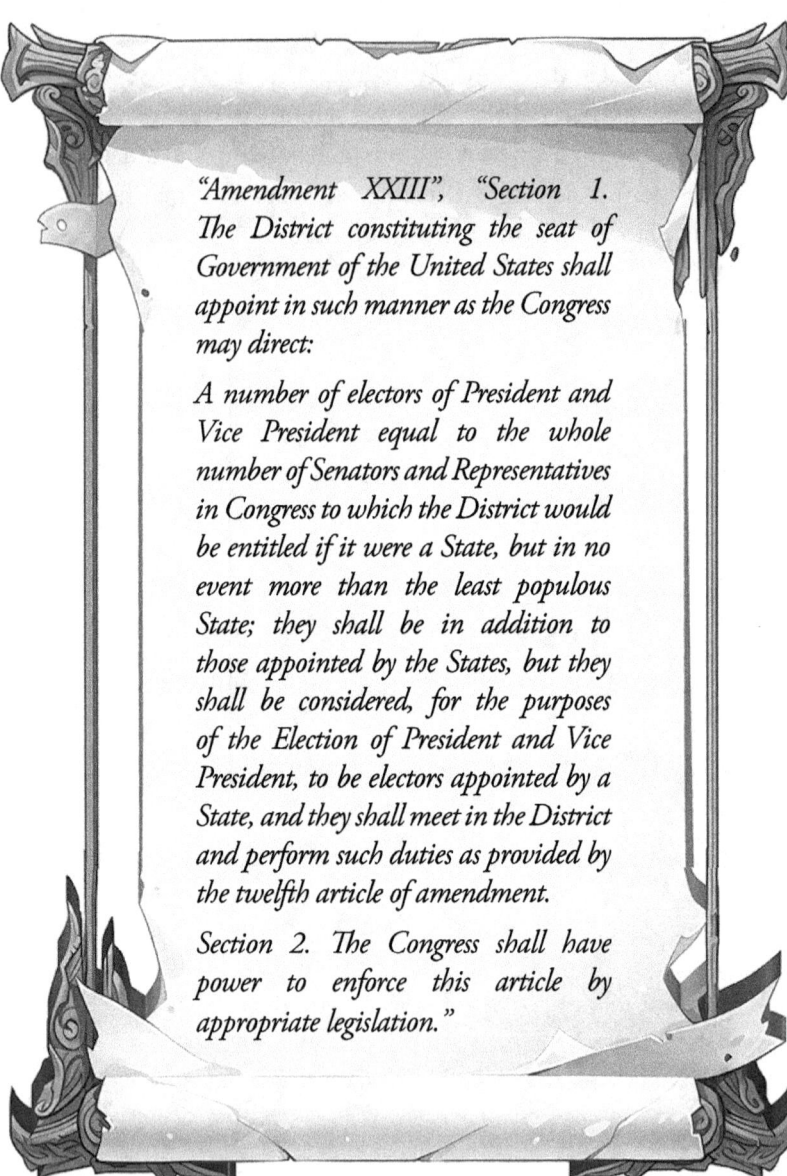

"Amendment XXIII", "Section 1. The District constituting the seat of Government of the United States shall appoint in such manner as the Congress may direct:

A number of electors of President and Vice President equal to the whole number of Senators and Representatives in Congress to which the District would be entitled if it were a State, but in no event more than the least populous State; they shall be in addition to those appointed by the States, but they shall be considered, for the purposes of the Election of President and Vice President, to be electors appointed by a State, and they shall meet in the District and perform such duties as provided by the twelfth article of amendment.

Section 2. The Congress shall have power to enforce this article by appropriate legislation."

Here we are allowing the District of Columbia to act as a state only for the purpose of having electors for the president and vice-presidential election.

Our founders were opposed to having the seat of government ever becoming a state. They believed if it did all the representatives would act as if they were from DC and not the state they were representing. They would move their families there and be effectively representing the seat of government, rather than the state which they were sent to represent.

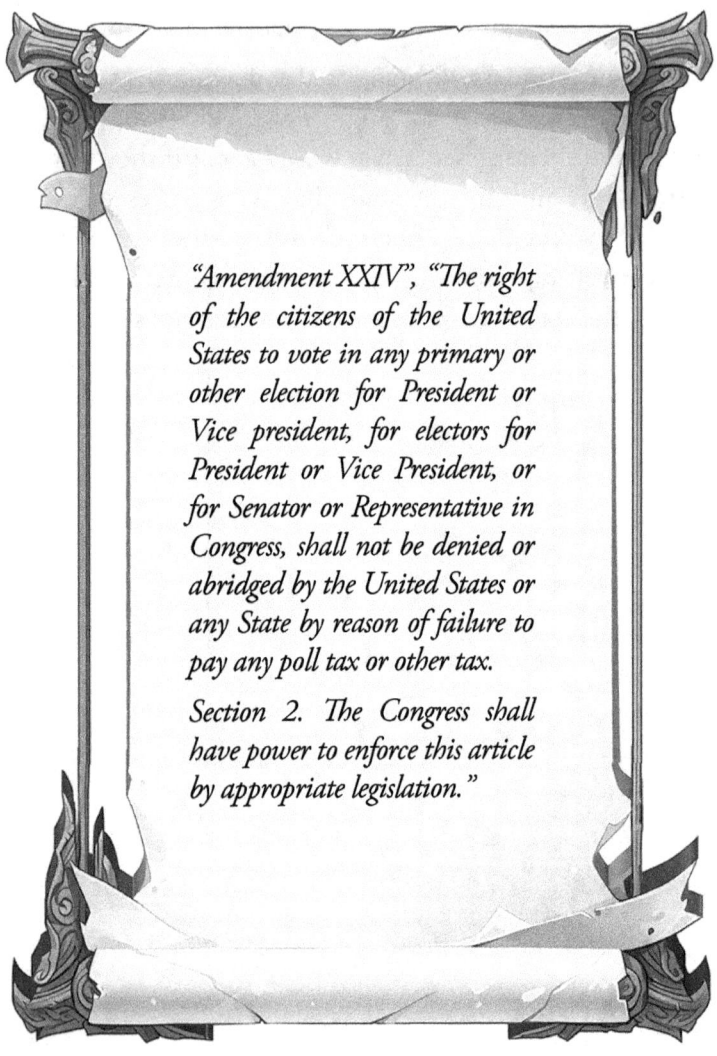

"Amendment XXIV", "The right of the citizens of the United States to vote in any primary or other election for President or Vice president, for electors for President or Vice President, or for Senator or Representative in Congress, shall not be denied or abridged by the United States or any State by reason of failure to pay any poll tax or other tax.

Section 2. The Congress shall have power to enforce this article by appropriate legislation."

Here we are restricting the state or federal government from instituting a poll tax or any tax for that manner in order to vote. There had been laws primarily in the south to stop minorities from voting. Many of these laws are referred to as Jim Crow. Our system does not allow restricting voting or paying people to vote either. No one can receive anything of value for doing so.

> *"Amendment XXV", "Section 1. In case of the removal of the President from office or his death or resignation, the Vice President shall become President.*
>
> *Section 2. Whenever there is a vacancy in the office of the Vice President, the President shall nominate a Vice President who shall take office upon confirmation by a majority vote of both Houses of Congress."*

Here we are once again dealing with the line of secession of the presidency. The vice president shall become president in case of removal, death, or resignation. Whenever there is a vacancy in the vice presidency, the president may appoint a vice president subject to approval by both Houses of Congress.

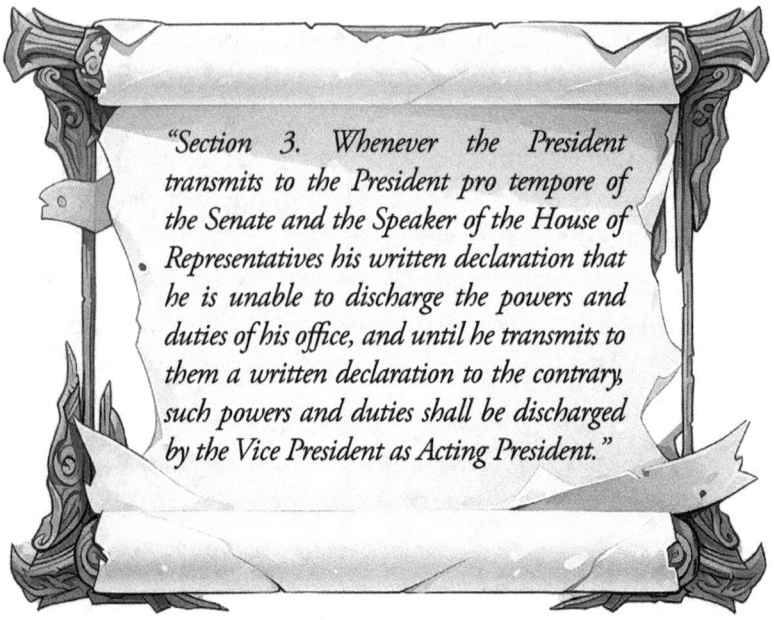

"Section 3. Whenever the President transmits to the President pro tempore of the Senate and the Speaker of the House of Representatives his written declaration that he is unable to discharge the powers and duties of his office, and until he transmits to them a written declaration to the contrary, such powers and duties shall be discharged by the Vice President as Acting President."

This provides a way to temporally step down as president in the event that he can't fulfill his duties, and it provides an avenue to take power back once he feels he is again fit to serve. He can deliver a statement to the president pro tempore of both Houses of Congress of the fact, and the vice president will fulfill his duties in the meantime. He can then, at any time, submit a statement to the contrary to take back his power as president.

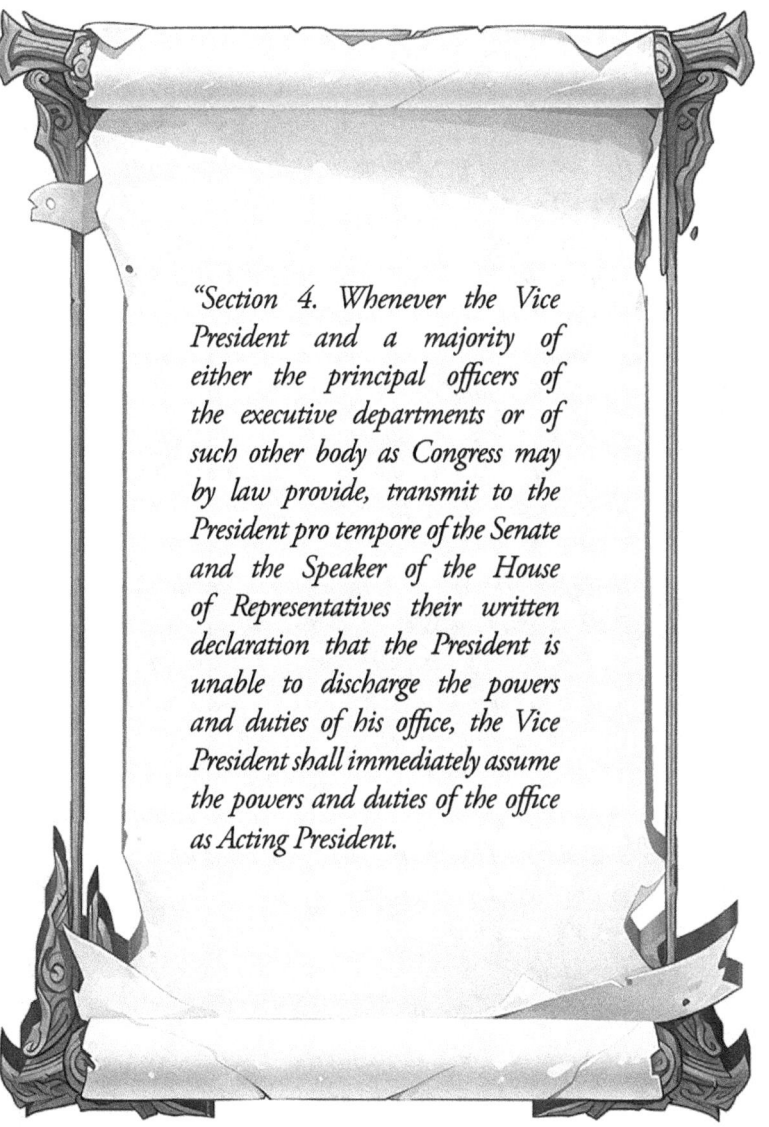

"Section 4. Whenever the Vice President and a majority of either the principal officers of the executive departments or of such other body as Congress may by law provide, transmit to the President pro tempore of the Senate and the Speaker of the House of Representatives their written declaration that the President is unable to discharge the powers and duties of his office, the Vice President shall immediately assume the powers and duties of the office as Acting President.

Thereafter, when the President transmits to the President pro tempore of the Senate and the Speaker of the House of Representatives his written declaration that no inability exists, he shall resume the powers and duties of his office unless the Vice President and a majority of either the principal officers of the executive department or of such other body as Congress may by law provide, transmit within four days to the President pro tempore of the Senate and the Speaker of the House of Representatives their written declaration that the President is unable to discharge the powers and duties of his office. Thereupon Congress shall decide the issue, assembling within forty-eight hours for that purpose if not in session. If the Congress, within twenty-one days after receipt of the latter written declaration, or, if Congress is not in session, within twenty-one days after Congress is required to assemble, determines by two-thirds vote of both Houses that the President is unable to discharge the powers and duties of his office, the Vice President shall continue to discharge the same as Acting President; otherwise, the President shall resume the powers and duties of his office."

This provides for the removal of the president of the United States should he become unfit to serve. A majority of his principal officers of the executive departments would have to submit a declaration to the president pro tempore of the Senate and the speaker of the House of Representatives to that effect. Congress may provide some other body and at such time the vice president would become the acting president. The president can deliver to the same that no such disability exists. The principal officers can again do the same, and Congress shall meet to decide the issue. Two-thirds would have to decide that the president is unfit to serve, if not, the president remains.

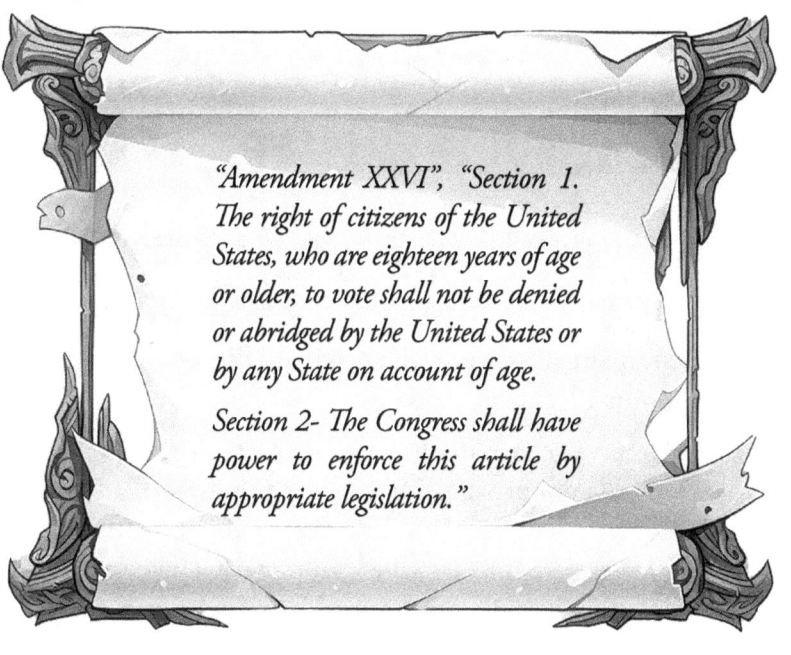

"Amendment XXVI", "Section 1. The right of citizens of the United States, who are eighteen years of age or older, to vote shall not be denied or abridged by the United States or by any State on account of age.

Section 2- The Congress shall have power to enforce this article by appropriate legislation."

Once again, pretty straight forward. Once you turn eighteen, you have the right to vote. Citizens could be drafted to serve in the military before they were given the right to vote. This amendment was passed to change that fact.

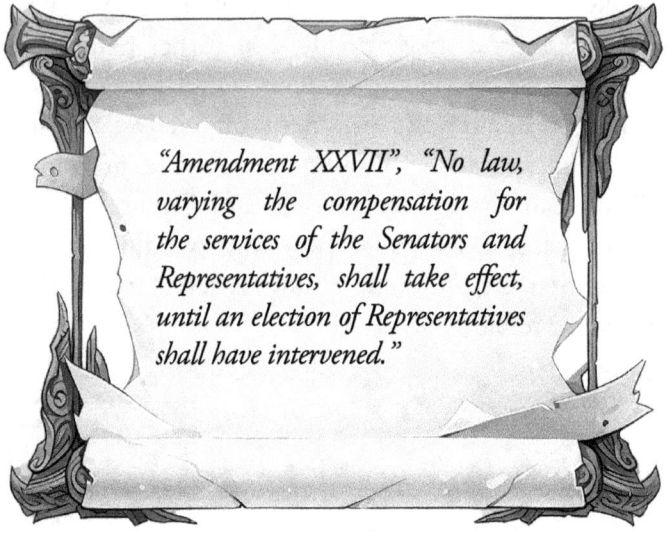

"Amendment XXVII", "No law, varying the compensation for the services of the Senators and Representatives, shall take effect, until an election of Representatives shall have intervened."

If Congress gives themselves a pay raise, they must face the voters before it shall take effect, by the next election of the House of representatives. This amendment was one of the original "Bill of Rights" passed in 1792.

Here we come to the end of the Constitution, so let's talk about what I haven't said. Roe vs. Wade, Brown vs. the Board of Education, or any other landmark decision by the Supreme Court. You might ask why? But in doing this, I have used the simple language of the Constitution itself. I am not saying I disagree with any of these decisions. But they are just that, decisions, and we've all seen decisions we didn't agree with. Over the years, some justices have inserted their beliefs, ruling one way or another for political reasons. Sometimes just looking at what the populous wanted, rather than following the absolute greatness of our founders, who argued for months to write from almost nothing but their wits and experiences to establish what has become proven to be the greatest Constitution on earth! So here I have gone where the Supreme Court always should, to the text of the Constitution, guided by the original understanding of the intentions at the time of its writing. This Constitution is, by the way, the oldest active Constitution on the planet and is so for a reason, the brilliance of its founders.

Of course, we also have our state Constitutions and basic law itself. So, in studying law, there is more at play. Although the federal Constitution is supreme in our system, followed by state Constitutions, should there be discrepancies, cases that maintain settled law, roughly still become the law of the land until they are overturned, which takes many decades at times if ever. I have not allowed unintended consequences to interfere with the work here at hand. Also, I want the reader to understand when referring to the Republican or Federalist parties, Republican in no way relates to today's Republican party. I have avoided using the term Democratic-Republican as it is not accurate and is used to explain the party rather than to be historically accurate. The term GOP refers to the grand old party, which leads back to Jefferson's Republican party. The name was chosen because of the reverence felt towards the old party, but I digress.

With that said, next, I would like to get into the founders that actually signed the Constitution. Knowing their lives and backgrounds helps to better understand how and why they came to the turn in the road they did. These are intended as a brief outline only.

Delaware's Delegation

George Read -

A Federalist party member, he attempted to reconcile with England. Became opposed to the stamp act as well as anti-import regulations that the crown passed. John Penn appointed him to the crown attorney general. He was a member of the Continental Congress. There he led what was called the court party. The court party was a group that was supportive of the royal court of England, but as time passed, he became disillusioned. Once reconciliation failed, he moved to establish American legal and political foundations. He voted against the Declaration of Independence which divided the delegation as only two were present and the third delegate had to be called in to break the tie. He was the President of Delaware's Constitutional convention. Delaware sent him as a delegate to the constitutional convention. While there he advocated for a national government and a new Constitution, he supported a republican form of government and the presidential veto power.

Gunning Bedford Jr. -

During the revolutionary war he was appointed Deputy Muster General by the continental congress and assigned to the Northern army in Canada to muster troops. Then reassigned to serve as aid to General Washington. He was Delawares attorney general and served in the congress of the confederation. During the Constitutional Convention he wanted only to amend the Articles of Confederation. He made what was known as his so called "small threat." Basically, some people would find foreign allies of more honor and faith who would do them justice, which was shouted down as treasonous by other delegates. He opposed population representation. A staunch defender of states' rights. Served on the committee that offered the grand compromise which held that one branch would be by population and the other by an equal number. He was a George Washington nominee to the US District court of Delaware, and he served until his death.

John Dickinson -

He wrote the 12 "Letters from a farmer in Pennsylvania." Was active in writing the Articles of Confederation. He was known as the penman of the revolution. He served as an officer in the American Revolution, was delegate to the 1st and 2nd Continental Congresses and was the author of the "Olive Branch Petition" which was the last attempt for peace with England. He wanted reconciliation rather than Independence, and he even refused to sign the Declaration of Independence, favoring some way to make peace. He did leave Congress and joined the militia. He was a slaveholder (Keep in mind this is a Delaware delegate) who freed his own and was a big believer in religious liberty. He was a Quaker and an active abolitionist. An unabashed abolitionist, during the convention he opposed the slave trade on moral grounds and moved to have it prohibited, which led to Article 1 Section 9. He also supported a strong central government.

Richard Bassett -

A veteran of the Revolutionary War, US Senator, Chief Justice of the Delaware's Court of Common Pleas, and Governor of Delaware. He became circuit judge for the 3rd Circuit and was a member of Delaware's Constitutional Conventions. He never spoke during the convention or served on any of the committees. He was nominated by John Adams to the 3rd Circuit. One of his midnight appointees and he served until 1802 when President Jefferson abolished his court. He was first a member of the Anti-Administration party, and later as the Pro-Administration Party. Basically, a faction in support or opposition of Alexander Hamilton's policies. These factions were forerunners of the Federalist and Republican parties.

Jacob Broom -

He was a dedicated supporter of a strong central government. He urged Washington to use his influence to begin a union of the colonies. He was a quaker and never served in the army, but he did draw up maps for Washington prior to the Battle of Brandywine. At the Convention he seldom spoke although he supported a President for life, Nine-year terms for Senators. He wanted the states to pay the representatives salaries, wanted congress to have the power to negate state laws and equal representation for the states. He was generally quiet in public but did speak from time to time in the Convention on things he felt were crucial. He was religiously active as well, described as "a plain good man."

Maryland's Delegation

James McHenry -

He initiated a resolution to form the Navy. Fort McHenry carries his namesake. He kept notes during the convention, served as the secretary of war during Washington and Adam's administration. During the Revolutionary War, he served as a surgeon and was a prisoner of War. He was appointed aide to the Commander in Chief and served as Secretary of War. He was elected to Maryland's House of Delegates where he advised against reducing the size of our armed forces, and he resigned from President Adam's cabinet in 1800 following infighting.

Daniel of St. Thomas Jenifer -

He had close ties with the colonial government and over-time he became much disillusioned with the overreach of parliament concerning laws of taxation and trade. He joined the cause for independence becoming President of Maryland's Council of Safety and represented Maryland in the Continental Congress. He worked to find solutions arising from the Articles of Confederation with Washington, Mason, and Madison. He attended the Mt. Vernon Conference, which led to the Constitutional Convention, where he and Franklin both enjoyed elderly statesmen status, he supported a strong and permanent union of states, and he often used humor and congenial contacts towards this end.

Daniel Carroll -

He was a slaveholder who joined the patriot cause. He served in the Maryland Senate and helped to raise troops and money for the revolutionary War. He fought the ratification of the Articles of Confederation until all the states ceded their land to the federal government. Maryland, his state, was the last to ratify the Articles. He was a believer in a strong central government and spoke out against states paying their members of Congress, believing that it would undermine the central government. He thought by doing so, the new government would become just another Continental Congress. He wanted a President chosen by the people rather than the legislature. A big believer in religious freedom and only one of two Catholics to sign the Constitution. He was a strong supporter of what became the 10th amendment; he supported the federal government assuming the states' debt and approved of the new federal government on the banks of the Potomac. Believing it should not be in any state.

Virginia's Delegation

John Blair -

A well-known legal scholar, he served as a Virginia Court of Appeals judge and a Supreme Court judge. He became an important influence on how the Constitution was ultimately interpreted. During the constitutional convention he was opposed to a single executive and wanted the federal government to negate state laws. He was known for cutting through the fog and getting to the heart of the matter. He was a devoted patriot, who was opposed to the stamp act. When parliament dissolved the House of Bourgeoisie, he worked to stop the import of goods from England until taxes were repealed. Blair called for a Continental Congress. He worked on the committee that drafted the Virginia Government Bill of Rights and he was a Washington appointee to the Supreme Court.

James Madison Jr. -

He was known as the father of the Constitution, and he was the 4th President of the United States. Well prepared for the Convention, he spent months studying self-government in his home on the upper floor, and he even wrote the Virginia plan. He got a list of all the delegates and worked to organize the list on the basis of who would support his new plan, he was well organized going into the convention. He served as the fifth Secretary of State under the

Jefferson administration. Often cited as the founder of the Republican Party, I would dispute this believing Jefferson is the founder. He owned a large number of slaves and was a member of the Continental Congress and helped to organize the Constitutional Convention. He was a close advisor to Washington, and he believed in religious freedom. He was against paper money and diplomatic immunity, and he worked with Randolph and George Mason to present the Virginia plan, which became much of our Constitution. He also kept extensive notes during the Convention, probably the main reason we know what happened.

North Carolina's Delegation

William Blount -

An American Statesman and land speculator. His family was big in the independence movement. He served as a paymaster during the Revolution and became involved in the defense of Charleston. Was a two-term member of the Continental Congress and pushed to open land for settlement west of the Appalachian's, helped defeat liquor and poll taxes. He was active in negotiating Indian treaties. As a delegate to the constitutional convention, he arrived on June 20th violated the rules of secrecy and took a copy of the Virginia plan back to congress citing that nothing would become of the constitution he later returned, and Gouverneur Morris convinced him to sign. He led efforts to get North Carolina to ratify the constitution. George Washington appointed him as

Tennessee' territorial Governor. And after statehood he became senator, he was involved in a conspiracy to seize Louisiana land with Great Britain. He was ejected from the senate and impeached by the house he was the first official to face impeachment.

Richard Dobbs Spaight -

He served in the Continental Congress and sat on a committee to examine the conduct of judges. Spaight proposed senators to be elected by state legislatures and he was in favor of the president serving a 7-year term. During the states ratifying convention in 1788 he spoke 11 times to convince his state to adopt the Constitution, but his attempts were made in vain. The Constitution was passed the following year in a different ratifying convention. He had prominent roles in education and religious affairs, and he served as Governor and a member of Congress as a Republican. He had a political feud with a Federalist that he ran against, which led to a duel where he was mortally wounded in the fourth round and later died of his wounds.

Hugh Williamson -

An American physician and Politician. He was elected to the Lower House in North Carolina. He worked to secure veterans' rights, and he wrote the state's copyright law. He served in the Continental Congress and was a champion of Federalism. Experiences during the War for Independence convinced him of the need for a strong defense and national government. He attended the Annapolis

Convention, a meeting of a group of central states. He was well versed in interstate issues. He roomed with Hamilton and Madison at the Constitutional Convention and was invaluable at hammering out compromises. He was elected to the first federal Congress and wrote letters in defense of a strong federal system. As a North Carolinian, he opposed slavery.

South Carolina's Delegation

John Rutledge -

An American Politician and jurist, He was one of the first associate justices of the Supreme Court appointed by President Washington and became the second Chief Justice, although he never heard a case in that role. He was a recess appointee who was later rejected by the Senate. He also served as Governor. He served as a delegate to the Continental Congress and delegate to the Stamp Act Congress, which protested taxes by Great Britain. During the Constitutional Convention, he served as chair on the committee of detail, which took what was passed and set it into a working document, probably the most important committee at the Convention. He is responsible for the Convention not outlawing slavery outright, probably because he was a slaveholder himself. He also suggested the executive branch be a single person. He stopped working in government due to rumors of a mental decline.

Charles Cotesworth Pickney -

He fought in the War for Independence in Pennsylvania, Florida, and Charleston. During the siege of Charleston, he was taken prisoner when it fell. He was a practicing attorney and served in the state's Lower House and its Senate. During the Convention. He advocated for a strong federal Government. He proposed that senators serve without pay and he fought to give the Senate the power to ratify treaties. He also helped in defense of the slavery issue. He was a federalist and was appointed to serve as a minister to France, but they refused to receive him because he refused to pay a bribe to a French official stating, "No, not a sixpence." He also ran unsuccessfully for President and Vice President. He was a charter member of the board of trustees to South Carolina College, as well as President of the Charleston Bible Society.

Charles Pinckney -

He served in defense of the nation and was taken prisoner and held on a prison ship for a time. He called out problems with the Articles of Confederation. During the Constitutional Convention, he spoke more than a hundred times on various issues. He believed strongly in protecting property rights, a central government, separation of powers, and was very concerned with the people's rights and religious freedom. He also stood in defense of slavery. He even presented his own draft of the Constitution known as the Pinckney Plan. He is credited for no religious test being given for serving in the government. He was for two branches of the legislature, the Houses power to impeach, a singular executive, power of raising a military to Congress, regulations of interstate commerce, and foreign commerce controlled by the Federal Government. He spoke so often he was nicknamed "Constitutional Charlie." He also served four terms as Governor. He served as Jefferson's state campaign manager and was a founding member of the Republican Party of South Carolina.

Pierce Butler -

He mobilized South Carolina's militia to fight against Britain's invasion. However, their troops were not as well trained as the British troops. When Charleston fell, he managed to escape and organized a counterstrategy and resistance. He had been a former Royal officer, and Britain believed there were more Loyalists in the South. The war left him poor, and he tried to reconcile with former loyalists. During the Convention, he wanted the president to be able to start a war and believed in a strong union. He introduced the fugitive slave law and supported the twenty-year prohibition. He served three terms as U.S. Senator, first as a Federalist, then as a Republican, and finally as an Independent. He hid out Aaron Burr on his plantation following his duel with Alexander Hamilton, in which Hamilton died. Following the Burr conspiracy, his political influence faded.

Georgia's Delegation

William Few -

He was appointed to Congress by his state's legislature in 1786. He served as a delegate to the Constitutional Convention; however, Congressional duties kept him away for much of the proceedings. He never made a speech there and missed all of July and some of August. Regardless of his lack of attendance, he is credited for getting the Constitution through Congress. He later served as a U.S. Senator and a federal judge. He also served in the New York legislature after moving there later. His remains were initially buried in New York but were later moved to Augusta, Ga., at the state's request.

Abraham Baldwin -

He was a graduate of Yale and later became a teacher there until he became Chaplain in the Revolutionary Army. After the war, he studied law and was admitted to the Connecticut Bar. He received a land grant in Georgia and moved there to open a law practice. The giving of land grants was common and was done to convince the settlement of land. He created a plan for secondary and higher education, and he believed that education was key to settlement on the frontier. He was elected to the Georgia legislature and obtained land grants for a university. During the Constitutional Convention, he served on the Grand Committee, where he was influential in getting "The Grand Compromise" between the competing plans through. Later he served in Congress and the Senate as a Representative for Georgia. Jefferson and Madison were close allies of his and they opposed Hamilton's ideas, a staunch opponent of his. He was considered the moderate leader of the Republican Party.

William Jackson -

He served in the war in Charleston and Florida. He was captured during the siege of Charleston. He was shipped to Philadelphia and held there until he was released in a prisoner exchange. He served on General Washington's staff as an aide, after the conflict when the constitutional convention was called for, he wrote to Washington asking to be considered as secretary. He served in that capacity chosen over Ben Franklin's grandson. So, he is the only signer not to be a delegate.

George Washington -

First in war, first in peace, first in the hearts of our countryman, Father of the country, what more can I really say. President of the Convention. A slaveholder that ordered his slaves freed upon his wife's death. He believed in a strong central government and was religiously active. He was our first president and as such, many numbers of firsts came from that role. He is the reason that presidents only serve for two terms, which is now enshrined in our Constitution. In fact, if not for him, we would have a king. He won us independence and tried to keep his life private on his Mt. Vernon plantation. In his farewell address he warned us about political parties. He even wrote the first proclamation for a public day of Thanksgiving. As the first president, he set about setting up a new government strictly following the Constitution.

New Hampshire's Delegation-

John Langdon -

A Staunch supporter of the Revolution, Langdon sat on New Hampshire's Committee of Correspondence, attended various patriot assemblies, and was a member of the Continental Congress. He built privateers for use against the British and was in one of the militia units in Saratoga at Cornwallis' surrender. He became speaker of the state's legislature and he even paid expenses for both him and Nicholas Gilman at the Convention because New Hampshire was either unable or unwilling to do so. They were late to the Convention and arrived at the end of July, but they helped to broker a compromise over the slavery issue. He was also a big believer in a strong federal government, and he spoke more than 20 times. He was first a Federalist who later became a Republican and he remained active in state politics until the end.

Nicholas Gilman -

He enlisted in the army and served until the end of the war. His family was very involved in the cause for Independence, and he served as a clerk in his father's store. Gilman also served in the Continental Congress. He was late arriving at the Constitutional Convention. He arrived in late July with John Langdon after much of the work had been done and made no speeches. He did, however, help get the Constitution through the Continental Congress. He served on the Committee of Postponed Matters late in the Convention. He was an important Federalist, but by 1804 he was an elected Republican and Jefferson appointed him as bankruptcy commissioner.

Massachusetts' Delegation

Nathaniel Gorham -

He served in the congress of the confederation and became President of the body, wrote a letter to the king of Prussia asking him to act as King of America. He was very concerned over problems with the Articles of Confederation. He also served in the Massachusetts General Court and delegate of the Provincial Congress. In the Constitutional Convention, he served as chairman of the Committee of the Whole, which made him often in charge of the sessions as Washington would open the Convention, and then step down from the chair. He also served on the important committee of detail. He had a reputation as an excellent administrator. He also fought hard to get the new Constitution through the Massachusetts Legislature.

Rufus King -

A leader in the Federalist Party as well as an attorney and diplomat. He served in the congress of the confederation where he introduced a resolution calling for a convention in Philadelphia with the direction to propose amendments to the Articles of Confederation. He served in the convention on the committee of style and on the committee of postponed matters. He wanted increased power for a central government. He worked hard to get his state to ratify the new Constitution. Later he moved to New York upon the urging of Hamilton and served as their Senator until Washington appointed him as Minister to Great Britain and continued in that capacity into Jefferson's administration. Later, he returned to the Senate and has the distinction of being the last Federalist candidate for the presidency.

Connecticut's Delegation

William Samuel Johnson -

He was a graduate of Yale and an honorary graduate from Harvard, though he really self-educated himself in Law. He passed the bar and practiced in both New York and Connecticut. Later in life, he became president of New York's Columbia College. He was a militia officer as well as serving in both the Upper and Lower House of the Connecticut Legislature. He had trouble choosing sides for independence and tried to play peacemaker. He arrived June 2nd at the Constitutional Convention, where he served on the Committee of Style and worked to get his state to ratify the new Constitution.

Roger Sherman -

He was well respected by his colleagues and had the distinction of signing the Articles of Confederation, the Declaration, as well as our Constitution. During the Convention, he proposed the Great Compromise, which gave us two branches in the legislature. This broke up a major log jam at the time. Many wanted either one or the other by state or by population. He was a Federalist and supported Hamilton's call for a National Bank, national road, as well as protective tariffs. At the time Hamilton proposed this, it created a great divide in Washington's cabinet and, more than anything, led to the creation of our two-party system.

New York's Delegation

Alexander Hamilton -

Founder of the Federalist party. He fought for a national bank, national road, was a brilliant economist, and the nation's first Secretary of Treasury. A confidant of Washington, he fought in numerous battles during the Revolutionary War. During the Convention he spoke against all the plans speaking for what he wanted some referred to this as the Hamilton plan, but he proposed none. He was one of the main authors of the Federalist Papers, if not the main one. His writings argued for the ratification of the Constitution in New York. He believed the Articles of Confederation would separate us and hoped for a strong union of states with a strong central government. We owe Hamilton greatly for a strong dollar because he fought to take on and pay all debt. He had a 3% plan to eliminate the debt, which was mocked. Jefferson resigned from Washington's cabinet over numerous disagreements with Hamilton, which is the big reason for our two-party system. He was killed in a duel with Aaron Burr, who was tried and found not guilty of murder. He had been Jefferson's Vice President, even though Jefferson and Hamilton were political rivals, but the duel was not Jefferson's doing. Hamilton died in his beloved New York City, where he's interned.

New Jersey's Delegation

William Livingston -

Livingston was a lawyer and founder of the first weekly paper called "The Independent Reflector," a Presbyterian publication. There were two other Presbyterians who founded it with him. They went after the founder of King's College, an Anglican, accusing him basically of conspiracy. He served in the continental congress but wasn't in favor of independence so in June 1776 he was recalled by his state. Serving in the constitutional convention he was a great advocate for a free press, religious liberty and against a state religion. He was made commander in the state's militia and was elected Governor in New Jersey.

David Brearley -

David was a captain in the Monmouth militia, Chief Justice of New Jersey's Supreme Court, and eventually a member of the U.S. District Court. Britain had him arrested for high treason for opposing an act of British parliament, but a mob released him. In the convention he supported the New Jersey Plan. He served as the chairman on the Committee of Postponed Items, which dealt with a number of things as they tried to hammer out a finished document. Later, he became a founding member of "The Cincinnati" a veteran's society.

William Patterson -

He studied law under Richard Stockton, who later became a signer of the Declaration. Patterson practiced law in New Jersey. He was a militia member and served in the Provincial Congress. He later became the state's first Attorney General. He attended the Constitutional Convention until late July, he proposed the New Jersey plan leaving unhappy with the direction of the convention. Returning apparently only to sign the document. He worked hard for ratification. Later, he served in the U.S. Senate and worked on the Judicial Act. He was an Associate Justice on the U.S. Supreme Court.

Jonathon Dayton -

He was a member of both the House and Senate, served as Speaker of the House, and was an important member of the Federalist party. As a soldier, he fought in numerous battles during the Revolution. Later, was a member of the Society of Cincinnati and served in the state legislature. He was the youngest member of the constitutional convention. He supported Hamilton's policies and helped to suppress the whisky rebellion. The city of Dayton is named in honor of him, and he has the distinction of being the youngest signer of the Constitution.

Pennsylvania's Delegation

Thomas Mifflin -

He served in the colonial assembly. He served as Pennsylvania's president and it's first Governor, as well as in the Continental Congress, he signed the continental association a document meant to limit trade from England, he was president of that body, which is why some want to recognize him as President. He even served on the board of war. He resigned from congress to enlist in the war. During the war, he was an aide to Washington, serving as quarter master. He was Pennsylvania's first Governor, and he presided over the committee which wrote the state's Constitution. During the convention he seconded the motion on the emolument clause, restricting payment by the federal treasury only.

Benjamin Franklin -

Referred to as The First American, he was the inventor of bifocals, the Franklin stove, and lightning rods. While testing rainwater, he found there was a problem with lead paint. He also is famous for his kite to key experiment. The printing press made him larger than life and wealthy. He authored and published the Poor Richards Almanac and assisted with a radical pro-patriot paper as well. He fought the Stamp Act, served as the Ambassador to France, the first Postmaster General, and was a signor of the Declaration. He was carried into the convention with a special chair with railings or rods attached as he suffered badly from gout. He believed in a strong central government and was an important Federalist. He called for prayers during the convention to help them get through the conflict which resulted in the great compromise. He was truly, at the time, one of only two aging statesmen there. He was also credited for putting our money on the metric system. He believed in a strong central government and was an important Federalist. It's important to understand many were Federalists at first and later became Republicans, as the Republicans became more for a stronger government than even the Federalist's were for in the beginning.

Robert Morris -

Opposed Britain's tax policy and the Stamp Act. He Served in the state's legislature and the Continental Congress. He served on the secret committee of trade responsible for funding the revolution and he personally financed or raised money for financing the war efforts. He is known as the financier of the revolution. He signed the Articles of Confederation as well as the Declaration. He rarely spoke in the Convention but worked hard for ratification. Washington stayed with him during the convention. He was Washington's first choice for Secretary of the Treasury, which he declined. He later served in the U.S. Senate, where he was a supporter of Federalist policies and Hamilton. He was engaged in land speculation trying to recoup the losses from the war and went broke during the financial panic. He served time in debtors' prison and he's why congress passed bankruptcy laws.

George Clymer -

He opposed the Tea Act and Stamp Act and was active in the protests in his state. He served in the state legislature, the Continental Congress, and the state legislature. In the continental congress he served on the board of trade and the treasury. When the city was evacuated due to the pending occupation he stayed behind with George Walton and Robert Morris. He was a signer of the Declaration. He was also a devout abolitionist, during the convention he served on a committee looking for a compromise over the slavery issue. He was later elected to the nation's first Congress.

Thomas Fitzsimons -

He was affected by the stamp act and fought the coercive acts as well. Served as a captain of the militia. In the constitutional convention he supported a strong national government and an end to slavery, he's one of only two Catholics who signed the constitution. Generally speaking, he sided with the federalist positions. As a U. S. Representative, he advocated for protective tariffs and retiring the debt.

Jared Ingersoll -

He served in the Continental Congress where he felt a growing need for a stronger government than the articles of confederation could give us. In convention, he first only wanted to propose amendments to change the articles but grew to accept the ideas of a new plan. He participated in all the sessions but seldom if ever, spoke or debated.

He became deeply partisan. He was so disturbed over Jefferson's election in 1800 and became the Federalist vice presidential candidate in 1812.

James Wilson -

Wilson was another member of the Continental Congress. He really became important in the convention, where he served on the committee of detail. He spoke for popular elections and was the main force in how the executive branch was set up. He wanted the legislature set up by population. He helped propose the 3/5ths compromise and fought the electoral college. He was a signer of the Declaration, and Washington appointed him to the Supreme court. He fought for ratification and was opposed to the Bill of Rights. There were many who opposed the Bill of Rights believing it didn't need to be spelled out, believing these rights were already there in the Constitution and therefore it was unnecessary.

Gouverneur Morris -

He was a signer of The Articles of Confederation as well. Served in the Continental Congress and became a spokesman for the Army fighting for their needs. He was very active during the convention and has been called the Penman of The Constitution, even writing the preamble. He supported the aristocracy and thought only landowners should vote, thought new western states should be admitted in a less than equal manner. He referred to them as backwoodsmen and thought they could offer little to the new country. He believed in unfettered religious liberty. He spoke in convention more than anyone else on almost everything. Spoke out against slavery, saying "A man can't be both man and property."

Now, at the end of the signors, I have not listed delegates who didn't sign. Some went home and fought ratification. I am not concerned with those because it doesn't explain the meaning of the document.

I must explain and give credit for much of this. I have studied much of my adult life on The Constitution and our founding. Reading first "*The Miracle in Philadelphia*", "*Debate on the Constitution*", "*The records of the Convention,*" some of what I've said came from education, tours of the founders' homes, as well as online sources. I have tried to be as accurate as possible forgive me for any errors there may be.

There are times when reading that you must understand our language has changed some in the 230 plus years. But generally speaking, you should be able to understand it fairly well especially living under it throughout your lives. I don't deny the abuse of it also, so keep in mind some of this is how it should be in an exact reading.

I really hope everyone takes something from the book, that instills conversations for a better understanding. It was my thought that it would be carried with you. I kept it brief for that reason. And put the exact original language of the Constitution in scrolls for easy reference. I sincerely hope this is used as a kind of reference book. So many times, I read an article from a major news source that is so wildly inaccurate, talking about what's in the Constitution when it clearly isn't, or elected officials trying to change things that would be clearly unconstitutional. Change is Constitutional if done through proper channels as prescribed by our founders two ways, by amendments or by calling for a new convention of the states. Both are hard bars to cross. Unfortunately, these incorrect notions make their way into public discourse. There are many of our representatives that haven't even read it, and schools no longer teach it. I have been told of people asking our elected officials if they've read it and being told they haven't. Keep in mind these people must take an oath to defend the Constitution of the United States, and usually the Constitution of their state as well. When we elect persons with no knowledge of our founding documents, obviously, it is ripe for disaster. Defense of our republic begins at home with the defense of our rights outlined here.

Most of our founders were successful simple citizens, sure they were mostly politicians of their time. But they were moved towards the cause of liberty They weren't interested in spending their lives in government just to be there, they had a reason, and that reason was the cause for liberty. They were fighting to self-govern themselves, it wasn't their intentions to have a career in government. They wanted to serve in order to achieve a better government and then go home to their plantations and lives. Serving in Congress was meant to be a temporary thing. Our early presidents even paid for their cabinet appointees themselves; some going broke in the process. What a difference that would be, it would sure be a smaller government.

In my mind. I really want the government we were promised. People talk about our Democracy. What I find so profound is that it isn't even a democracy. We are a Democratic Republic. We elect people to make decisions on our behalf, wherein a democracy you would be voting on every bill - all of us - that's why democracies fail because over time, people grow tired of constant activism. Great men do not create great events, Men become great because of great events and their ability to react to them. -